P9-CFF-310

My
Tender Soul

A Story of Survival

PEGGY L. MCNAMARA

Beaver's Pond Press

Edina,   *Minnesota*

Although this is a true story, the names of participants and locations have been changed to protect anonymity.

Copyright © 2000 by Peggy L. McNamara. All rights reserved. No part of this book may be reproduced in any form whatsoever, by photography or xerography or by any other means, by broadcast or transmission, by translation into any kind of language, nor by recording electronically or otherwise, without permission in writing from the publisher, except by a reviewer, who may quote brief passages in critical articles or reviews.

ISBN 1-890676-61-6

Library of Congress Catalog Number: 00-102326

Second Printing: August 2001
Printed in the United States of America.

04 03 02 01   5 4 3 2

Beaver's Pond Press, Inc.   5125 Danen's Drive
Edina, Minnesota 55439-1465
(952) 829-8818
Fax (952) 944-4065

Table of Contents

Part Three: *The Road Home*

Acknowledgements

Never in my wildest dreams did I think that I ever would write a book. Now that it is completed, it seems as if it was only a matter of destiny. As I reflect on this process, it seems that this message was always in my heart, and yet it would have never come to fruition without guidance, support, encouragement and love from many people.

The first person who I need to thank is someone who is not really involved in my life anymore. His name is Dave Muller, and he is the person who first suggested that I should write a book a few years ago. As I was making a transition from my former line of work to my new professional speaking career, Dave was there to help. When he first mentioned the idea of my writing a book, I laughed at him. Well, Dave, you were right on. Without your suggestion who knows when, or if, this would have been created. For that encouragement I am eternally grateful.

Another person who was brought into my life at just the right time is Annie Slawik. I don't believe I would have had the courage to complete this project without her guidance, support and belief in me. Annie is one of those people who gives to the world with no expectation of receiving anything in return. She read and re-read my story to make sure it was cohesive and yet communicated the message that I wanted it to. Annie, you are a true friend. My life would not be the same without you.

The Greer family has become important to me. Not only has Kathy become an irreplaceable co-worker, our relationship has also become an irreplaceable part of my world. I refer to her as "my gift from God." Kathy came into my business two years ago and has worked countless hours, with little pay, to promote my programs. I don't know what I did to deserve her. She is always willing to lend a helping hand to anyone who asks for it. I know that she and her family will always be there to offer advice or open my eyes to a new opportunity whenever I need it. Kathy, I have grown pretty attached to you and am thankful for everything you have done for me.

I met Diane Hart a few years ago, and am I ever glad that I did! She has been my graphic designer and go-to person for marketing ideas, style and vision ever since. This book would not have come together as nicely as it did if it weren't for her ideas for the cover design. Diane, you always know just what I am looking for and you do it so well. I treasure our friendship and working collaboration.

One other person that I feel compelled to mention is Milt Adams. For all practical purposes, Uncle Milty has become a mentor of mine. I don't think it was ever planned that way and yet, serendipitously, it has happened. My book would not have been completed in a timely fashion without your guidance and assistance. Milt, from the bottom of my heart, thank you for all the time and energy you have put into this project.

There are countless other people whom I could include that have encouraged my decision to go ahead with this book. I am just going to offer a generic "thank you" and trust that the receivers will know how grateful I am for their help. This is for those of you who have offered advice on the technical end, suggestions on content, offered encouragement and supported me through prayer. I do appreciate everything that has been done for me.

Last, but certainly not least, I want to thank my husband and my son: Pat and Jeremy. They have put up with my long hours, mental distractions and financial adjustments to support my business and my message. It has not always been easy, and yet the three of us know in our hearts that it has been worth it. Jeremy, thank you for being the sunshine on gloomy days and keeping me on task by asking about the progress of my book. Pat, thank you for talking with me and calming me when I've awakened at 3:00 A.M., panic-stricken by all the challenges that lay ahead of me. Thank you for holding me when I need to be held, for loving me when I need to be loved and for being my best friend. I love the two of you with all of my being.

Welcome

Writing a book about one's life is a daunting task. I have struggled with many emotions while creating this: self-doubt, bewilderment, fear, vulnerability, excitement, clarity, apprehension, urgency, anger and love. I am sure there are many more, but these are the ones that come to my mind immediately.

While this is a story of overcoming many obstacles, it is also a guide to helping you make the most of your life—whatever you want that life to be. One of my favorite quotes is from Galileo, who said, "You can never teach a man anything, you can only help him to find the answers within."

I am not trying to teach you anything. I certainly do not have all the answers, but I have learned some things that I feel compelled to share with you. This book will help you find the answers within, *if* you are willing to seek them.

You see, it takes a willing heart to foster personal enrichment. It takes a willing heart to expect the best out of life. It takes a willing heart to find inner peace, joy and fulfillment.

The challenge, for me, is that I can't give you "a willing heart," or passion for inner growth, or the desire to improve your life. However, once you recognize a need for the above-described qualities, then I can offer you a helping hand.

Welcome to the journey of My Tender Soul. I am grateful for the trust you have offered me by allocating your time to read this, thankful for the energy you will put into this message and thrilled to have you become a part of my life.

Enjoy the road,

Prologue

Saturday morning, June 19, 1999. It's 7:00 A.M. and I'm standing on the front steps of my home, still in my pajamas, waving good-bye to my father. He had come up from his home in central Missouri for a quick visit, and now he is heading back. His duties as a minister make it hard for him to get away for long periods of time, so we've only had about 36 hours together, but we made the most of it.

As I watch him drive away, I feel a broad range of emotions. It is hard to clarify exactly how I feel; I am overjoyed that he was here, yet I feel tears of sadness starting to well up in my eyes as I watch him leave. I close my eyes, take a deep breath and remind myself to be thankful for the time we had together. After all, at one point in my life I couldn't have imagined spending even five minutes visiting with my father, yet we just had a day and a half together. He had enjoyed seeing the Mall of America for his first time, touring Hastings and noting how it has changed over the years, and socializing around the bonfire in our back yard last night. I remind myself that, yes, it was a good visit.

Upon opening my eyes I see the sun is just coming up over the horizon. The birds are singing their morning tunes, my plants and flowers are blooming, and there is a fresh coat of dew on all the area lawns, and I start to relax. I have been a bundle of nerves since I found out that dad was coming to visit. That was about two weeks ago, and as the days went by, I found that my ability to concentrate on anything became virtually non-existent. I have been so pre-occupied, and so tense, that I am now starting to feel the effects of it.

I open my front door, head back inside, and allow myself to begin to cry. My husband is already back in bed, my son is still sleeping and I decide to take advantage of the quiet time; to think and reflect and ponder. I grab a blanket and my journal and head to one of my favorite spots, the recliner in the living room. It sits in the corner of the room, surrounded by three large windows and I find it very soothing. I sit down, get myself all settled and begin to take care of my tender soul.

Part One

The Early Years

Chapter One

I was born into a typical, small-town, mid-western family in 1967. I was the second child, the first daughter, in a family that came from a long line of hardworking country folk. Both my parents had grown up on farms. My mom grew up on the same farm that her father had been raised on. Her grandfather, my great-grandfather, had come over to America from Czechoslovakia when he was 19 years old. He ended up settling in Minnesota, where he bought the chunk of land that she called home. Mom was the younger of two daughters. There also was a boy who died as an infant a couple of years before mom was born.

My father was the oldest of three children and the only son. He had grown up in central Minnesota. His father was a farm hand. They lived in the country and worked for area farmers. My dad was a junior in high school when the family moved to Meadowbrook. That is where he met my mom.

Dad was average in height, on the thin side and, but for his crooked teeth, would be considered handsome. He had sandy brown hair and a constant smile on his face. He was known for being a bit rambunctious, which would be typical for a farm boy, but he would never do anything to hurt someone intentionally.

My mom fit the stereotype of a small-town girl. She always wore a dress, had a great smile with pretty white teeth, dark hair and a pleasant face. The pictures I have seen of her at that time of her life show me a person that I never knew. She seemed carefree and fun loving. I have been told that she dreamed of being married and having children. Mom's older sister, Edith, was the more dominant of the two girls, and mom has spent most of her life trying to emulate Edith. It somehow never happened.

Mom and dad were high school sweethearts and were married shortly after graduation. The year was 1961 and it was a time of ideals. Expectations of life were quite a bit different back then. The husband was, typically, the breadwinner and the wife stayed home, raised the kids and everyone was supposed to live happily ever after.

My father took a job doing the only thing he knew: selling farm equipment. He and mom had their first child in 1962, a boy they named Nathan. He had dark hair, dark skin, brown eyes and was tall and lanky from the beginning. My understanding is that, from the very first day of his life, he was a momma's boy, the kind of kid who stayed inside to play and hung close to his momma's side.

When I was born, in 1967, my brother was not thrilled to have another child in the family. He had been an only child for five years and didn't like the attention switched to someone else. As far back as I can remember it seems that Nathan always resented my presence. I can't put my finger on any specific event and yet, somehow, I could just feel the hostility.

I have had a stubborn streak in me from the beginning of my life. When I was a baby, mom would try to feed me vegetables and I would just spit them back out at her. She would try to hide them in different-flavored baby foods, but it never worked—right back out they came. I had light-colored hair that had a bit of a curl to it, a chubby face and small features. I was the smallest, and most obstinate, of mom's babies. Apparently, I even potty-trained myself; I must have been tired of waiting for someone to teach me and decided to take care of it on my own.

Nathan was more like our mom, while I took after dad. While Nathan hung out with mom, I hung out with dad any chance I could. Our life changed in the fall of 1969, when another boy, Timothy, was born into our family. Timothy was, and is, as completely different from Nathan as anyone could be. As a baby, he had pale skin, blond hair and big blue eyes. His cheeks were full and he had a belly that was quite chubby.

Tim became my pal. We were close in age, he had more of a laid-back demeanor than I did, and he would always listen to me. That made him my kind of kid! I could get him to play with me where Nathan never would. Nathan became more distant, not only because of our age difference, but also because he didn't like the additional competition Tim represented.

In the spring of 1972 the fourth, and final, child was born, another girl. She was named Jessica, and she became the new baby of our family. The largest of all of the babies, she was just over 10 pounds at birth. I did not know what to think of this baby that mom and dad brought home. They had laid her in the middle of their bed, we three kids lined up at the edge staring at her in awe. She was chubby, bald and didn't do too much other than cry. I think Nathan was more enamored with her than Timmy and I were.

Our family was complete. Due to dad's work, we moved around Southern Minnesota quite a bit—in fact, each child was born in a different town. Nevertheless, the family ties remained strong; even with all of our moving around, we never lived farther than a couple hours away from either set of grandparents. Most Sundays were spent with one side of the family or the other, playing cards, visiting and eating lots of food.

I certainly don't recall all of the different places that we lived. I have heard from various sources that our family moved between eight and fifteen times by the time I was five years old. However, I do know that one of our stops was Hastings, Minnesota, the town that I currently live in.

My husband grew up in Hastings, and we have lived here since we were married in 1992. On one of our many summer bike rides, I went searching for the home I lived in when I was a child. I had an idea where it was, and I found it on Fifth Street West. It is still there, a 1½-story home that was built in the 1940's. It has a one-car detached garage and a fence that still surrounds the back yard. I remember it as being brick red, but it is not that color today. When we lived there we had a German Shepherd, King, that Timmy and I loved to play with. We would spend hours with him in our back yard.

We lived in that house for almost a year and the one Christmas we spent their was the year Santa brought me a green kitchen play set. I had wanted one so very much and I was trying to be on my best behavior and not beat up Tim too much the month or so before Christmas. I was so excited as I came downstairs that Christmas morning and saw the kitchen set sitting by the tree!

My role as a devoted daddy's girl wasn't affected at all by Jessica's arrival. Interestingly, it was only recently that I recalled that this was the type of relationship that we'd had. I was my father's tag-a-long friend, a tomboy from the very beginning, and was always anxious to ride along with him, in his truck, whenever I could. It didn't matter what the occasion was, whether it was to sell farm equipment or make deliveries, I liked the adventure it offered.

Chapter Two

Within a few months of my memorable Christmas, when I was 4½ years old, we were packing up, getting in the car and moving again. This move happened in a hurry—we didn't even have a chance to finish painting my bedroom before we left. A sad difference from our other moves, though, was that this time we couldn't bring King. He had recently bitten the milk-man, and my mom and dad had him put to sleep.

I tried to understand what was happening in our world, and yet couldn't quite comprehend it at that age. We were moving to central Missouri, which was about a twelve-hour drive away from "home." My father was transferring there to work with a long-time friend at a Massey Ferguson (farm implement) shop. This was to be the first time my parents had been away from their families. My mom's parents did not like this idea at all. They felt from the beginning that it was a mistake to move so far away.

We settled in a small farming community similar to the ones we had left behind in Minnesota. To this day there still are gravel roads throughout town. The only paved road is the main one running through town.

I am sure the move was tougher on my mom than my dad. She has always been very close to her parents and sister. In fact, I would say she has been dependent on them for most of her needs her entire life. They made her decisions for her, formed the opinions she was supposed to have and turned my mom, Barb, into someone who did not know how to take care of herself.

Being so far away meant that we no longer had the weekly family gatherings. Mom couldn't just pack us kids into the car and go for a quick visit to her parents. She couldn't just pick up the phone and call whenever she felt like it. She had never expected to move away from her hometown, or at least the surrounding area, and now she was 500 miles away.

~

It was time for me to start kindergarten and I couldn't wait to go. Nathan always hated school and dreaded going, and he just could not figure out why I wanted to go so badly. I couldn't wait to learn new things, meet new kids and to have something useful to do with my time. I felt so important going off to school.

The only thing I didn't like about it was that I could no longer spend as much time with dad as I wanted. He worked long hours and would usually have some free time in the afternoons. Well, I went to school in the afternoon and hated missing out on seeing him. He worked six to seven days a week, and I would go down to the store with him any time that I was allowed. I spent hours at that store with him, going on sales calls with him, making delivery trips or just sitting in the office and playing on the typewriter while he was on the phone. I was the only one allowed to go with him and I reveled in it. Nathan was not interested and the other two were too young. It made me feel special to be the chosen one.

One evening we four kids were pulling ourselves up to the supper table and I noticed that dad was gone for supper again. That never used to happen. Dad had always made it a point to be home for supper, but lately that wasn't the case. We were seeing less and less of him as the weeks went by.

Mom was standing by the counter, frying hamburgers in the electric skillet. We were anxious to eat and started grabbing at the food that was already on the table. Mom told us to settle down and seemed a little shorter on patience than she usually was.

Her hair was wrapped in curlers, she had on the typical polyester slack and floral shirt, and she was still carrying around those extra pounds from us kids. She had always worn eyeglasses, and the style at that point was, the bigger, the better. I looked at her as she unplugged the fry-pan, brought it over to the table with her spatula, and started to serve us our hamburgers. Being the vocal one in the family, I asked, "Mom, where is dad?"

She looked at me, gave Timmy his hamburger, slammed the spatula down onto the fry-pan, and said, very angrily, "Well, he is probably out for a drink again with Shelly," and left the room.

Nathan looked at me with a scoff and told me I shouldn't have asked where dad was. I didn't mean to upset mom, I just wanted to know why dad wasn't home again. I helped myself to my hamburger, Nathan fed Jessie and the four of us ate in silence.

I had no idea what mom meant when she said what she did. I asked Nathan to explain it to me and he wouldn't. He didn't want to talk about it and I knew not to press mom any further. As a five-year-old, I couldn't tell what was going on between my parents. I didn't know that asking a question would get mom so mad at me. I didn't know why we saw less and less of dad every day.

⌒〜

The next thing that I knew was that, one week shy of finishing the school year, we were packing our belongings to move, again. This seemed like another quick decision and yet, for all I knew they could have been planning it for some time and never told us.

I came home from school one Friday afternoon and was told to go up to my room and pack my things, because we would be taking off very early the next morning. I asked where we were going and I was simply told, "We're moving." I asked where, and I didn't get an answer. I asked about school and was told that I was going to miss my last week.

I didn't know what was happening, and yet it seemed pretty serious. I asked a few more questions but received no answers. Instead, I was told, rather sharply, to just get up to my room and to watch over Tim and Jessie. I grabbed those two and headed upstairs. Nathan was in his room and I tried to ask him what was going on, but he shut the door in my face. I don't know if he even knew where we were going or was just upset because he didn't want to move again.

I was anxious about the move; I still didn't know where we were going, and I had a hard time falling asleep. I knew I had to get up really early the next morning and be on my best behavior, but I just couldn't sleep. I had tried that entire afternoon to question mom, but she wasn't talking. Dad was in a bad mood and I figured I should just stay away.

The next day, as we were getting situated in our car, I found out we were going back to Minnesota. The furniture was still in the house and I was told that dad would make another trip to come back and get it. We had been gone for less than a year and my parents decided it was time to go back home.

I am not sure that either of my parents had a plan for this move. It was a long, quiet drive and I slept as much as I could. I was tired of being in the car, squished between my siblings, and I wanted to know how much longer we'd be driving. When we crossed the Iowa-Minnesota border I was told it would only be a little longer before we reached my grandparents farm.

We went directly to Grandpa and Grandma Baker's place—my mom's parents. I always loved visiting their farm. They owned about 80 acres and grandpa did most of the work himself. He raised corn, wheat, alfalfa and beans. They had 17 milk cows, 8 calves and a whole bunch of chickens. My great-grandpa, (the one straight from Czechoslovakia), still lived on the homestead. He had an orange trailer at the bottom of the hill, south of the driveway, just below the house.

As we turned into the long driveway heading up to the house, we kids were rather jubilant. Our parents were not. At that moment, I wasn't aware of the negative mood in the car and yet, in hindsight, I know it was there.

Dad parked the car and the three older kids jumped out as fast as we could. Mom trailed behind with Jessie in her arms and dad brought up the rear. Grandma came out of the house, walked down the porch steps and came to meet us. She had been drying dishes; still holding the towel in her hands, she greeted us sternly.

Grandma is a rather short, stout lady with legs as big as tree trunks. She wore her hair in a typical no-nonsense style and rarely had a smile on her face; on that day, her demeanor was especially severe. She did not appear happy to see us at all. It kind of stopped me in my tracks. She stood there, with her hands on her waist and began to chastise my dad. My mom, still holding Jessie, went and stood by grandma, and Nathan followed her; Timmy and I stayed by dad.

Grandma kept saying over and over again, "I told you not to take Barb and the kids down to Missouri, how could you do such a thing?" "What are you going to do now?" "You should have listened to me." "I told you this was going to happen."

The tirade seemed to last an eternity, although in reality it was probably only for a few minutes. I didn't know what was going on. Dad told us kids to get our things out of the car and take them inside. This confused me because I thought we were just stopping by here for a visit, but I knew better than to question his demands at this point. Little did I know that my life was about to change dramatically.

~

When our things had been taken out of the car, dad told us to crawl back in and get settled because we were going to go for a drive. The next thing I knew, all six of us were back in the car and heading down the driveway, away from grandma's.

At the end of the driveway, dad turned right and then took another immediate sharp right. He was driving into a cornfield and parked our blue rambler on the edge of it. He told us kids to get out of the car and we did. Mom was crying uncontrollably.

I grabbed my little sister and pulled her onto my lap as I sat down on the ground. My two brothers sat beside me, one on each side. Mom had gotten out of the car and she was sitting way off to the side of us. We kids were looking directly at dad, who had stayed partially in the car. He was sitting in the driver's seat, turned towards us with his left leg on the ground, his right arm sitting over the steering wheel.

I was waiting for somebody to say something. It wasn't happening, so I finally asked what was going on. Mom told us, between sobs, that our father was leaving us and heading back to Missouri. I looked at her and said, "Yeah, dad is going back to Missouri to get the rest of our things."

Mom looked at me and said, "No, your father is going back to Missouri to stay." I looked at Nathan, and he didn't say anything. I looked at dad, and he sat there with his face down. I looked at mom, and she was very upset and was crying even harder.

I didn't know what to think. I didn't understand why he was leaving us. I looked at dad again, and this time he looked up at me; staring directly into his eyes I said, rather matter-of-factly, "I don't want my daddy to leave."

I will never forget the look on his face after I said that. It was one of remorse, anguish and helplessness. He looked so sad, and yet he never replied to my statement. He just looked away.

Chapter Three

All of a sudden, my grandparents had new roommates. I feel that God always looks out for us, and most of the time we are not even aware of it. I'm not sure what would have happened to us if my grandparents hadn't been there, or if they hadn't been willing, to help us pick up the pieces of our shattered lives.

My mother was completely devastated by this. I don't believe she had any idea that this was coming. This kind of thing didn't happen in the family that she had been raised in. Nobody, on either side, had ever divorced before. In her mind, marriage wasn't supposed to end.

Yet there she was with four kids, no job skills, and no clue as to how to provide for herself or her family. My dad, or her parents, had always been there to take care of her. She had never held down a job before; she'd never paid a bill and knew nothing about budgeting for a household.

After dad left, mom became virtually non-existent to us. She cried and cried and cried for days on end and rarely left her bed. I did my best to stay out of her hair and was trying to help grandma out where I could.

Timmy and I became inseparable, and we spent our summer playing at the farm. Jessie was only a little over a year old and too young to join us, and Nathan was still not interested in being with us. He stayed inside with grandma and mom most of the time.

One of our favorite things to do was to go see the man who lived on the other side of the pasture. His name was Arvid Mann. He lived alone, in a little old one-room shack, and he drank a lot. At least that is what grandma told us. He was probably drunk any time we went to visit him, but we weren't aware of it. He had some great stories to tell, and I found him just fascinating. I had never met anyone like him before. He didn't have any family, had never married, wasn't the cleanest guy around, and yet I sure liked going down there. I think part of the attraction was just the excitement of getting away with something. You see, even though grandma told us to stay away from him, I would sneak down there any time I could, dragging Timmy with me.

My grandparents took over our lives. They were the caretakers, the disciplinarians and the support for my mother. Grandpa was a fun-loving, easy-going man. He was of average height and rather thin, with a balding head. Grandma definitely ran the household; presumably that is the way he wanted it. He spent most of his time out working on the farm.

One of my responsibilities was to go to the chicken coop each morning to gather eggs. I would grab the bucket from the basement, run out to the coop and, always with a little twinge of fear, open the door to go in there. There were chickens fluttering around everywhere, and they would occasionally peck at me. I was very careful when I reached in to grab those eggs. Some of those hens would get pretty angry with me.

I also had the job of running down to get my great-grandpa for supper each evening. This was the one meal that he ate with us each day. I would run down the hill to his trailer and knock on the door. He couldn't hear very well, so I never waited for a response. I would just knock, slowly open the door and enter—with a little trepidation.

His place kind of gave me the creeps. It had an "old-person" smell to it, which I suppose was just some moth-balls, but man, that odor hit me square in the face every time I opened the door. I would walk down the dark hallway to the living room, where I'd find him sitting in his rocking chair, with an afghan over his lap, watching television. The scene never varied. He couldn't speak English, so I have no idea whether he could comprehend what was happening on the shows he watched, but I suppose they must have offered him some entertainment.

Like his house, great-grandpa himself always seemed intimidating to me. After all, he was close to 100 years old and I just couldn't imagine anyone being that old. Whenever I could coerce Tim into joining me, I would make him go in first.

Invariably, as I entered the living room great-grandpa would look up at me and give me a half-grin. Due to the language barrier, I would have to motion with my hands for him to come up to the house. I am sure he knew what my presence meant, yet he would still sit there, staring at me, until he was good and ready to get out of his chair.

After a few moments, he would slowly get up, put his afghan over the back of the chair, turn the television off and start to make his way down that dark hallway that I hated. As soon as we were both out of the trailer I would start to run up to the house.

We had a big hill to walk up, and I don't know how he made it every day, but he did. I also don't know whether it was from fear or impatience, but I always ran ahead of him and was at the supper table, with clean hands, before he even made it into the house. I have no idea how he felt about that routine we went through every night. I hope that he understood my reactions. I was always glad that grandpa took him back home after dinner and I didn't have to repeat that scene twice in one day.

It's funny what people remember about their past. For example, I recall that out at the farm house the phones were on an old party-line system; a group of homes in the area shared the same phone line. Grandma would get terribly upset when the neighbors listened in on her phone conversations.

I also recall the mice that would sporadically find their way to the main level of the house. I was scared to death of those little creatures. There were plenty of cats around to control their population, yet every once in a while, one managed to sneak by.

The first kid to see the mouse usually started screaming. We would jump up onto chairs and yell for grandma to come and save us. She would come running, with a broom in hand, ready to kill that little scoundrel. Watching her chase a mouse around the house was quite humorous. Of course, we weren't any help; we probably just aggravated the situation.

Grandma loved us the only way she knew: by setting rules and making sure we were fed and clean. Grandpa loved us by playing jokes and tricking us. He tried many times over to get Jessie to eat a chicken bone. He'd laugh and laugh whenever he stuck a leg-bone into her mouth and she would just sit there and suck on it. He thought that was the funniest thing he had ever seen.

Occasionally, Tim and I would help grandpa feed the cows. We would sit on the back of his pick-up truck and push the hay bails off. One time, we both fell off with a hay bail. Grandpa kept on going and we were running and screaming for him to wait up. We thought he didn't know we fell off. Well, he knew, and was getting a kick out of watching us run from his rear-view mirror.

My grandparents did what they could for us, and for that I am eternally grateful. It could not have been easy to have their daughter and four grand-kids move into their two-bedroom farmhouse with them. They had their own pressures from life, and we added more. They were now responsible for their daughter and her kids. They did what any parent or grandparent would do—they took care of us.

Mom had no choice but to go to the County Welfare office and ask for help. We started receiving cash assistance, medical assistance and food stamps. It wasn't much, but it sure did help the situation. My grandparents were not wealthy people by any means, and having four kids in their home took a lot of extra money.

〜〜

That fall, when school started, I went into a state of panic. I was afraid to go. At the farm, with my brother Tim, I was still myself. However, beyond those confines I went from being an outgoing tomboy to a scared little girl. I had loved school the prior year, and yet I was terrified of going to first grade. I pleaded with grandma to let me stay home, but yet, obviously, I had to go.

Every morning, as the school bell rang, I would go into class, find my seat and wait for the day to end. My desk was, thank goodness, towards the back corner of the room, and I would sit there and fervently hope and wish that I would not be called on—for anything. I never raised my hand or volunteered to help. I was incredibly shy and afraid to talk to anyone. I was afraid of looking stupid.

Everyone already knew that my parents were divorced and that we were on welfare. I think we were the only family in town in that situation. At least, it felt like it. In that small town, where my mom grew up, news traveled fast, and I didn't want any further attention brought my way.

Grandma was responsible for getting Nathan and me to school every day and for picking us up afterwards. Mom didn't have a car, so she stayed at the farm with the two younger kids. Grandma learned, rather quickly, that she needed to be right on time to pick us up when that school bell rang and we were dismissed.

During the first week of school, she was a few minutes late one afternoon. It really upset me and she ended up finding me standing at the corner of the schoolyard crying. I wouldn't talk to anyone who had tried to help me before grandma showed up. I just sat there and cried. At that time, I had no idea why I responded the way I did. Now, I realize I was afraid of being deserted again.

As time went by I realized that my teacher was very nice yet I still hated going to school. I especially hated recess. I didn't know anyone, but they all knew who I was. I was given a stigma and felt humiliated. Many times I would stay inside rather than going outside with the kids. I was tired of being picked on due to my family situation; a situation that I was ashamed of, even though I had no control over it.

One day, during my inside recess, my teacher, Mrs. Hanson, tried to talk to me and I started to cry. I have no idea what she said to me, I just recall the tears starting to flow. I couldn't say anything; I tried and no words would come out. Mrs. Hanson sat by me for the entire break and helped me clean up my face before the other kids came back in. Nothing was ever said about that day, by either one of us. She may have told grandma, but if she did I never knew about it.

I had never cried at home, and now this was twice during the first months of school that I found myself in tears. I hadn't cried at all when dad left or through the summer months without him, and I didn't know why I was acting as I was now. My teacher did everything she could to make me feel comfortable and accepted in class. She did her part; I just didn't do mine.

Later that fall, 1973, my grandparents bought a house in town for us to live in. There just wasn't enough room for all of us out at the farm. Mom had no financial means to purchase or rent anything, and they bought us a place on the south edge of town just off Highway 74, which ran through Meadowbrook.

The house we moved into had lots of room to play. It didn't have a garage, but that didn't matter because we didn't have a car. The only neighbors we had were two families to the west of us, and a farm implement dealer across the road.

Our back yard was an acre in size, and just beyond the property line there was a set of railroad tracks. There was also an old shed (with creepy spiders in it) and lots of trees. Tim and I spent hours upon hours exploring back there.

Now that we were in town, we also needed some type of vehicle. Grandpa and grandma couldn't be running in from the farm to take care of our every need. In addition, the school bus wouldn't come out to our house to pick us up or bring us home. In those days, town kids did not have bus access. We weren't out far enough to be considered rural and yet we were quite a ways from the school. If it was nice enough we could walk, but on those cold Minnesota winter days, we needed some type of ride to school. Mom had no financial means of purchasing a car, so my grandparents helped out again and bought one for us.

Within a couple of months of living in our new home, right before Christmas, we had some visitors. It was a Saturday, shortly after lunch, when a car pulled into our driveway. We looked out the window and didn't recognize the vehicle. The only people who ever came to our home were our grandparents or mom's sister and her kids. We strained to see who it was, and I was shocked when I saw my dad and his parents climb out of the car. We became really excited and told mom who it was.

Within moments, they knocked on the door and mom answered. The minute that mom answered our door I ran to my bedroom, slammed the door, locked it, stood against it and did not move.

I hadn't seen dad since he had left us about eight months earlier. During that time, I learned very quickly never to ask about him; mother became very upset if we did. Since the day he left, my under-standing was that he was gone and that I should just forget about that side of my family; in fact, grandma had recommended that I com-pletely wipe them out of my memory. She said it would be better that way.

As mom opened the door to see them, she started crying and screaming. I am sure her face turned red, because it always did when she got mad like that, and I could hear some nasty things coming out of her mouth. Her tone of voice would become shrill and there was no reasoning with her whatsoever when she got this way.

I heard dad tell her that he just wanted to see the kids for a few moments and bring us some Christmas gifts. Mom didn't want to hear anything from him. She was oblivious to his needs.

The other kids stayed out there and I was straining to hear what was going on. I suppose my dad had asked where I was, because I heard mom specifically say to him, with an odd note of pride in her voice, "Peggy doesn't want to see you." The tone of her voice was hard to explain: almost like she was happy to hurt him in any way that she could.

There were some other things being said that I couldn't quite hear. My heart was just racing. I wanted to see my dad something fierce, yet I just couldn't force myself to leave my room.

The entire visit lasted maybe five minutes. As I heard the door close, I cautiously opened my door and walked tentatively to the living room. Sure enough, he was gone. Mom was sitting there crying and my siblings were standing there looking baffled.

Dad had left lots of presents for us, and I don't think any of us knew if we should be excited about having them or not. We didn't even know if mom was going to allow us to keep them. She did.

I was given a little set of china. It included teacups, saucers, sugar and cream dispensers and, of course, a teapot. I was never allowed to play with it because it was so fragile. Mom did keep it stored away for me, and about eight years ago she finally decided I could have them in my home.

Mom was upset for quite a few days after dad's visit. I was feeling sad and yet, I never allowed anyone in my family to see my hurt. I was always the strong one. Nathan moped, but I was determined to be strong for Jessie and Tim. Besides, I didn't want to disappoint my grandma by letting her know how much I missed my dad, and I knew that if I ever shared my feelings with mom she would be really mad at me.

For many years I was baffled by my behavior that day. I have since come to realize that I must have been more upset than I consciously knew with my father. After all, he was my buddy and he left me. I have since learned that, at one time, I had him wrapped around my finger. I guess I could crawl into his lap and pretty much get anything I wanted from him. I must have been devastated when he left us.

I don't remember the devastation, though. I don't recall ever being allowed to mourn or grieve or deal with the situation. How would I, a six-year-old, know how to handle it on my own? I did what grandma told me to and put away all my feelings, in an internal box somewhere, and locked it up tight.

～

The only people we saw, outside of school, were family. We spent a lot of time with our cousins. Mom's sister, Edith, had five kids and lived only about a half-hour's drive away from us, so we got together quite often. Our lives were certainly different from theirs, yet at that age, we didn't realize it. Our grandparents treated the two families quite differently. I am sure, in many ways, we were a burden to them and my cousins were not.

Grandpa and grandma were responsible for us and not for our cousins. We were consistently compared to Edith's kids. They were the "good" family; Edith married a business man and their kids were well behaved. We were the family that had gone through a divorce, was on welfare and needed all sorts of assistance from our grandparents.

Grandma and mom wanted me to be a young lady. They encouraged me to be more like Edith's daughters, my cousins, and I fought it. I was still a tomboy at heart and I didn't like being told what to do. I don't ever recall getting along well with my mother. I do remember trying to get some of her attention, and to make her proud of me; nevertheless, I argued with her consistently.

In addition to being withdrawn, I was not a very cute child. I needed glasses and we had to get the small black squarish ones because they were the only ones that the welfare system would provide.

My teeth were really crooked, but we did not get approval from the county for braces until I was 13 or so. All of my clothes were either hand-me-downs from my cousins or something that mom had sewn for me.

My stubborn refusal to eat certain food was still strong and kicking, but now it was powdered milk I objected to instead of vegetables. The dry milk was part of the food ration that we received from Kent County. I was so sick of drinking that stuff that many nights I would go without eating because I would not drink the glass that mom put in front of me—if I didn't drink the milk, I didn't get my meal. If she ever left the table, I would quickly dump the milk down the kitchen sink. Of course, I didn't get away with it very often because I had brothers who liked to tell on me. To this day, I can still remember the smell and taste of that awful stuff.

In second grade, my love for school was rekindled. Mrs. Johnson was my teacher and I worked really hard to please her every single day. She brought me out of my shell a little bit, yet I was still very shy.

We were learning how to print, and I was pretty serious about that task. I had a blister on my index finger from trying so hard. I still didn't like to go out for recess and now, I had a reason to stay inside: it was to practice my printing.

I did not want any attention directed towards me for any reason. In fact, I wouldn't even ask for permission to go to the lavatory. Once, that reluctance cost me. I had to go badly, but I was too afraid to ask to go. I hated raising my hand and having everyone look at me. Besides, it was the end of the day and I was sure that I could make it until I got home. I was wrong. I ended up peeing in my pants, sitting at my desk, just before the bell rang. I didn't know what to do. I tried to hold it and I couldn't.

When the bell rang, my plan was to stay seated until everyone was gone. However, one of the first kids to get up saw the puddle on his way out. Of course, he announced it to the entire class and I sat there, frozen, not knowing how to react. Mrs. Johnson looked at me, gave me a knowing, compassionate look and scooted the kids out of the room. She said she would get the janitor up here right away and told me to go on home and not to worry about anything.

Chapter Four

In the spring of 1975, when I was just shy of being eight years old, another change took place in our lives. Our mom was getting re-married. She had been dating a divorced man, from town, for about a year or so. The day we met him we had to be on our best behavior; we were lined up in the living room anxiously waiting to meet the man who was going to be our new "dad."

Tim, Jessie and I took to him right away; Nathan was more aloof. Brad was a middle-aged man of average height and weight with thinning black hair that he tried to disguise by pulling some long hair over the balding spot. His three kids from his first marriage were all around Nathan's age, so he was definitely starting over again. Brad had a big heart that attracted us immediately.

Mom was really excited about getting married again. It was nice to see her smiling and enjoying life. The Friday before the wedding, Mrs. Johnson announced the big event that was happening in my life that weekend. I hadn't told anyone about it and I had no inkling as to how she knew; I didn't yet realize how fast news travels in small town U.S.A. I was acutely embarrassed when the entire class turned to look at me. Nobody really knew what to say and I certainly was not happy about the attention that was brought my way.

The day of the wedding was the first time in a long while that I had thought my mom looked pretty. She wore her favorite color dress, mint green, and she was re-married in the same church in which her first wedding had taken place: the church that she grew up in.

It was a small wedding and we joined our relatives in throwing rice at the bride and groom as they exited the church. I don't think any of us really knew what lay ahead for us; I do know, however, that I was thrilled to have a "family" again. Mom seemed happier than I had seen her in years, and we were now part of mainstream society again due to the fact that we had a "dad." Nathan never really connected with our step-dad, while Jessie and Tim accepted him as the only father they knew. My reaction was somewhere in between.

Shortly after the wedding, we were packing up to move again. Brad had an older two-story home, closer to the center of town, and it was decided we would all move in to his home. Grandpa and grandma were set to retire from farming, and they moved into our home. After all, they were the ones who purchased it for us.

Brad's home was a bit outdated, and mom had the entire main level of the home remodeled right before we moved in. She was thrilled to make Brad's home into ours. She had the kitchen entirely gutted and re-created, the carpets changed and the bathroom expanded to make it twice its original size. Our new home also had a screened front porch, a back porch where we put our new dog, Buster, and three bedrooms upstairs.

Things seemed to be improving for us. Brad embraced us as his own children and did his best at providing for us. He worked at a company in Deerborne for most of his working life, and at this point he was on the night shift. He worked from 11 P.M. to 7 A.M., slept during the day and spent suppertime and the evenings with us.

Mealtime in our household was a loud, sometimes crazy, event. We were always picking on one another and were very competitive. We also had fun, and I can remember several instances when one of us would get to laughing so hard that milk would come spewing out of our noses and mouths. Many nights, I had to sit at the table long after everyone else had been excused, because I still had not learned to eat my vegetables. Our dog Buster got lots of great meals whenever mom turned her back on me.

We were so competitive with each other that Tim and I would have contests to see who could eat more than the other. Those contests usually involved pancakes, and I believe I held the record at 13—and mom always made large pancakes, so we are not talking about the little nickel-sized ones. It didn't matter how full I was, I was not going to lose to a boy—especially when that boy was one of my brothers.

I believe those were very good times for my mom. She was finally living some of the life that she had expected she always would. Besides being busy running our household, she now had a bit of a social group. People around town were more accepting of all of us. She and Brad joined a Saturday night card club that switched locations each week which created hours of fun for us. When it was mom and Brad's turn to host it we were allowed to stay up later because of all the commotion going on. People never left before midnight, and it was a good excuse to stay up late.

Nathan was our babysitter whenever they went out. He hated this assignment and often took his displeasure out on me. I do have to admit, though, that I probably didn't help the situation any, because I was pretty "lippy" towards him. My punishment was running up and down the steps 50 times, being grounded to my bedroom or losing my television privileges. This made me even more antagonistic towards him, and it seemed as if it became a vicious circle.

Brad really enjoyed the outdoors, and he decided that we should explore the world of camping. One October he bought a small pop-up camper and took us on our first camping excursion. We joined a large group of his work friends on our first trip. Naturally, it snowed on us, but even though we were all pretty cold, we found the trip to be quite a bit of fun.

Starting the next spring, most weekends would find us at one of the many campgrounds in Southern Minnesota. It became a family affair; my Aunt Edith and her family started coming with and, before long, my grandparents bought a camper and joined in the fun as well.

Within a year or so we graduated to a nicer and bigger pop-up camper. The more trips we had in the rain, the more we wanted to go up another level, and we ended up purchasing a Mallard trailer. It was olive green and we spent hours upon hours playing cards in that thing. Uno was the favorite one for all of us, especially grandma. She loved to win at cards and derived great pleasure from beating anyone that she played. She was a poor loser, and we knew that we'd better not rub it in if we happened to win.

Every Fourth of July we would take a two-week vacation somewhere up north. We chose a different spot each summer and created some great friendships with people. I found my first boyfriend on one of those camping trips.

His name was Sean and I thought he was the most gorgeous boy on this earth. I was 13 years old and he was 15. Sean had dark hair, dark skin and a trim body, and he treated me like a princess. He was much more sophisticated than I was about relationships, and I found that I was quite nervous around him. The closest I had ever been to a boy, besides my brothers, was when I slow-danced with Scott Carlson at a Sadie-Hawkins dance at school. During that slow dance I am sure there was three feet of space between us. You know, the old hands-on-the-shoulders rocking back and forth. That was the closest I had ever been to any intimacies with a boy.

Sean and I spent most of those two weeks together, swimming and lying on the beach. He kissed me a couple of times, and I am sure I was very inadequate. I hated to see that vacation end. It turned out, though, that Sean only lived about an hour away from us. We spent the rest of the summer writing back and forth to one another. Some of the letters I received from him were pretty romantic. He was pretty good at professing his "love" for me.

Before school started I talked mom into taking me to visit him. Tim and Jessie were pretty good friends with his younger brother and mom enjoyed the company of Sean's mom, so it was a relatively easy sale. Sean and I ended up, alone, in his room. This made me very uncomfortable. He tried to get me to do more than just kiss, but I was not interested. That was the end of my summer romance.

For entertainment in the winter, Brad bought a couple of snowmobiles. Nathan wanted his own snowmobile and bought a new one. The six of us spent many weekend afternoons out on those things. The times I enjoyed most were when I was able to drive a snowmobile myself or with a passenger. I loved to go fast, and several times I ended up throwing my passenger off the back end. It was great fun because it was usually Tim who went flying.

One of our snowmobiles had a throttle that stuck occasionally. This would create havoc for whoever happened to be driving it at the time. One afternoon as I was driving it through a ditch with Tim as my passenger, we went over quite a large bump that knocked both of us off the snowmobile. As we fell off, the snowmobile's engine did not quit, because the throttle was stuck; it just kept on going. Luckily, Brad was not too far behind us when it happened. He checked to see if we were all right and then took off after the runaway snowmobile. He did eventually catch it and stopped it before any damage was done. We were just rolling with laughter.

Even though our lives changed dramatically after mom married Brad, some things stayed the same. I still fought quite often with my mother. The older I got, the more I fought her attempts to mold me into a young lady like my cousins. I had my own personality and was angered whenever she would try to change it. It just didn't seem that we saw eye to eye on anything.

The first holiday season that we were in our new home with our new family arrangement, some visitors showed up at the door. This time, though, my dad wasn't one of them. It was only his parents who had braved the uncertain reception of my mother. I hadn't thought about my father for quite a long time. I didn't know where he lived, what he did for a living or why we never saw him. For that matter, I didn't even know where these grandparents or any other members of his family lived.

My grandparents had come to drop off some gifts and to see us for a few moments. Mom was in the kitchen; Jessica, Tim and I were in the living room watching Saturday morning cartoons. Our step-dad was upstairs sleeping, and Nathan was in his room listening to music.

There was a knock on the front door. We were a little surprised, because we hadn't seen or heard anyone drive up. The doorbell was outside the screen porch, so I figured it must have been someone we knew for them to come into the porch and knock on the door.

I jumped up to see who was coming to visit. I opened the door slightly, looked out and my heart stopped. Grandma Dean looked at me and said "Hello Peggy." I looked at her and grandpa and was puzzled because I didn't really know who they were and yet I had an awful feeling in my stomach. Before I had a chance to respond, mom appeared right behind me.

In an instant, the others were also standing by the door to see who was here; within moments mom pushed me out of the way and sent all of us up to our rooms. We stood on the steps so that we could listen in. Mom was yelling profusely at them with that shrill tone to her voice and I am sure her face was red and her hands were flying in every possible direction.

Grandma tried to talk to her, but had no luck. Again there was no reasoning with mom when she was in that state. Grandma said "Barb, we haven't done anything to those kids." The sad thing is, it didn't matter. In mom's mind anyone related to our father was to blame for the situation that had happened a few years earlier. She hated anyone, and everyone, involved in my father's life.

Mom ran them out of the house, and their gifts went, too; this time, mom would not accept them. As our grandparents started to leave, I ran up into my bedroom so I could look at them out my window. Of course, Jessie and Tim followed and we stood and watched them as they got in their car and left. I felt remorse, but, at that point in my life, I couldn't explain my feelings. Grandma Dean had seemed so nice as I opened the door, yet I knew that mom would be very angry with me if I told her that. I couldn't talk to anyone about them and so I just chose to put the whole episode away. Besides, any time

I would ask Nathan about dad or his parents he would get upset himself and defend mom and her reaction so, it just seemed better not to bring it up.

I only remember my grandparents coming to visit one other time. It was around the holidays again, and this time, mom chased them away with a baseball bat. They were never allowed to see us, nor were we allowed to see them.

As I grew a little older, and a little braver, I decided to pursue my quest for information about our father again, through my mom. Her reaction was even worse than it had been in the past. Sometimes I would get the belt because I wanted to know what happened or where he was. Other times the end of the fly swatter would come out. Sometimes, she would just scream at me.

Eventually, I gave up trying to learn anything about dad from my mom. I tried Grandma Baker, but whenever I asked her about him, she just told me to put those notions out of my head and forget about it. I didn't understand the situation. I just knew I felt scared whenever those grandparents came to the door. Sometimes, when we were home alone, we would dig in boxes to find old pictures of our dad. We knew right where mom kept the old photos, and we did our best to put everything back the same way we found it.

Chapter Five

I became very studious after I learned to read. I loved reading and spent hours upon hours doing that. I would make Tim and Jessie play "school" with me. I also had that kitchen play set in our basement and spent lots of time down there playing house.

Tim and I still spent lots of time together along with one addition: our tag-a-long sister Jessie. Mom made us take her with us. We would bring her with us on our ventures, until she ended up crying over something and then we would fight about who would have to take her back home. We found some neighborhood kids to play with and spent countless days playing baseball and football. I was the biggest of all the kids, most of whom were Tim's age, and I reveled in my power with them. It was my moment to shine.

Through elementary school I was kind of a loner. I had one good friend, Lisa, who was quiet, rather shy, a good student and—the real plus—she was nice to me. But we never spent time together outside of school until seventh grade or so, when we were 12 years old. As I approached that age I was becoming more outspoken towards my mom and actually became rather obnoxious. That, I suppose, is typical of the adolescent personality. I was not as withdrawn as I had been and was more open to having friends in my life. Little by little, I was coming out of my shell and as the year went on, I got involved in volleyball, basketball and softball. At that time, these were the only options for a girl who wanted to be in sports.

In the fall of 1979, the year that I had just entered seventh grade, we were going on another camping trip. That time of year can be beautiful in Minnesota and we took advantage of the nice weather as much as we could. As usual, Grandpa and Grandma Baker joined us, along with Aunt Edith and her family.

We arrived at the campground late one Friday afternoon. By the time we got everything set up, ate our supper and finished the dishes, it was dark and too late to do any exploring around the campground. Saturday came and about mid-morning the "women" decided to go for a walk around the grounds. Naturally, I was included in this group whether I wanted to be or not. I tried to stay at our site, but I received one of those piercing looks from my grandma and decided that I would just go along to keep the peace.

As we started out, Edith was near the front of the pack to lead the way. Her two daughters were next to her, grandma was a bit behind them, and mom, Jessie and I brought up the rear. Before too long, Edith grabbed the hands of her girls and they walked hand-in-hand the entire morning.

Within a few moments, mom grabbed our hands to hold them. Jessie, who was only about seven or so, clamped her hand within mom's. I had a different reaction and yanked my hand back as fast as I possibly could. There was no way that I was going to walk around the campgrounds holding my mom's hand. Besides, she had never done anything like that before or displayed any love or affection towards me that I can remember. I was just angry that, once again, she expected me to be like my cousins.

My early teen years were, like everyone else's, a time for gaining independence and hanging out with friends. I kept myself pretty busy, things were going along pretty good for us, and I didn't need to be around home much, so I wasn't.

Consequently, I didn't really notice that things were changing at home between mom and Brad. After working and spending time with the family, the only thing Brad really did on his own was bowl in a winter bowling league. Because he worked the night shift, he was in a league that bowled early Wednesday morning. It was his "time with the boys" and he would occasionally have a little too much to drink before he came home. Mom definitely did not like that and she would get pretty angry when he came home a little tipsy. I am not sure what she was actually angry about—was it that he was doing something without her, or that he'd have a couple of drinks, or just that she wanted to be angry at someone?

Meanwhile, mom was visiting her doctor with increasing frequency. She seemed to always have a doctor's appointment for something or other. As long as I can remember, mom has had this need, or desire, to see her doctors more than was actually necessary. She would make an appointment for any little ailment that affected her, or for that matter, us kids.

As we were growing up and becoming less dependent on her, these appointments gave her a reason to get out of the house. The thing is, though, she started to really dress up whenever she went to see her chiropractor. Not at first, just within the last year or so. She would put on makeup, jewelry and the nicest clothes she had to go see this doctor of hers. It seemed a bit odd to me, but I was pretty engrossed in my life and didn't pay much attention.

In the spring of 1981 Nathan graduated from high school. He never really liked school and couldn't wait to be done with it. He didn't have any big plans for his life, he just wanted out! The evening of his ceremony mom, Brad, Grandpa and Grandma Baker, and Edith and her husband, Bob, attended. Tim, Jessie and I stayed home with our cousins. We heard the big news when they got back home; the Dean family had come over to see him graduate. My dad's parents and two sisters, with their families, came over to view the ceremony. Mom seemed to take this "visit" in stride, but I sure could tell that Grandma Baker was flustered.

That summer, Nathan moved out. He had been working at a restaurant/bar in a little town called Clark, which is not to far from Meadowbrook, and he decided it was time to start his own life. I had mixed emotions when he left, although I would say the main one was exhilaration; it would be the first time in my life that I wouldn't be subject to his unpredictable wrath.

My freshman year started without a hitch. It was exciting to be this age, 14, because it seemed that there would be more freedom available. Lisa and I had our eyes on a couple of guys, and we were starting to finally gain some respect from the upper-classmen of our school. Mom had given her approval for me to wear make-up, and I had used my money from babysitting to buy some clothes that were "in style".

I walked to Lisa's house to pick her up every morning before school. She lived within a block of the school and this ritual allowed us extra time to hang out together before the bell rang. One morning that September, of 1981, my life was about to change once again.

I got up at my usual time of 6:30 to shower, eat and get ready for school. While I was in the bathroom curling my hair, Nathan came in to talk to me. I was surprised to see him home and thought he was just dropping by to get something. One look at his face, though, and I knew it was something else.

He was home to tell me that Brad was going to move out that day while we were in school—Mom and Brad were getting a divorce. They had gone to visit Nathan the previous night to tell him about their plans before Brad went off to work. They then asked him to tell the rest of us. I don't have any idea how far in advance this was planned or if it was something that happened spur-of-the moment, but I do know that I was in complete shock. I had no idea this was coming.

In hindsight, I think it is incredible that I didn't realize this or know about it, especially when I think of the strong communication my husband and I have with Jeremy. How could they not have said something to us? Brad had been my "dad" for seven years and suddenly, that day, while I was in school, he was going to move out without a good-bye to any of us!

I had known that mom and Brad argued occasionally, but what marriage doesn't have its challenges? Sure, money had been tight, but we were still receiving financial aid through the county in the form of medical assistance and food stamps. It wasn't a lot, but it had to have helped. I asked Nathan what happened and he said he didn't know. It's funny, but I don't recall seeing mom that morning. She must have stayed in bed. Brad wouldn't be home from work until 9:00 or so and of course, I had to leave for school around 7:30. Before I left, I told Jessie and Tim what I had just learned.

The walk to school that morning was rather melancholy. I didn't know what to do, how to react, or what to think; I felt numb. I got to Lisa's and walked through the garage to enter the side door of her home. I didn't even bother to knock anymore. It had been our routine for so many years that it was just expected that I would come walking through that door about 7:50 A.M. As usual, she was sitting at the kitchen table waiting for me.

School didn't start until 8:15, and we always took a few moments to chat before we left.

We were talking about girl things and I was trying to work up the nerve to tell her what I had just found out. Her older sister Mary was blow-drying her hair in the hallway and her mom was standing in the kitchen doing some dishes. I did not want to publicize the news and so I wrote her a note and handed it to her.

She looked about as shocked as I had been when I found out about an hour earlier. She didn't know what to say and neither did I. Her dad had recently passed away, so she would understand living in a single-parent family. We just kind of sat and looked at each other until it was time to leave.

We only had to walk a block to get to school, yet it was filled with lots of conversation. Lisa was asking all sorts of questions that I couldn't answer. I was in a daze and not looking forward to the day ahead of me.

By lunchtime, the news had already spread around the school. My entire class consisted of about 75 people. The whole school, grades 7 to 12, included only about 400 kids. Needless to say, gossip will spread like wildfire in a small community, and it did that day. Of course, nobody knew what to say to me, so we simply avoided the conversation in its entirety. I acted as though I could handle this and it was no big deal. I refused to shed a tear, or to let anyone see that I was hurting that day. Lisa saw a glimpse of it that morning, but beyond that, I appeared to be the same person I had been the day before.

I was dreading going home and was thankful there was something scheduled after school.

Cheerleader tryouts were coming up, Lisa wanted to go, and a group of us met in the gymnasium to practice. My intention was to go, watch and be moral support for Lisa; we were inseparable and it didn't matter what the event was, we always attended together.

While we were waiting for the coach to show up, our group sat in a circle on the gym floor, talking away. I kind of sat on the edge and just listened. I was so ashamed that my step-dad was leaving. None of my other friend's parents were divorced, especially two times. It seemed as if nearly everyone in town already knew everything about our lives, and now this happened. Any time someone looked at me it was with sympathetic eyes, but I could also tell they were thankful it wasn't happening to them.

When the practice was finished, I went back to Lisa's with her and stayed for a few moments. I didn't want to go home, but I knew that I had to eventually and so I decided I may just as well get it over with.

We talked Lisa's older brother into driving me home and they both wished me luck as I exited the car. I had no idea as to what I was going to see when I walked through that front door.

As I entered, Jessie and Tim were sitting in the living room watching television and mom was making supper. Nathan had stuck around until we went off to school that morning and then went back to his apartment and his life. Brad was packed and gone. He took only his clothes and personal items, leaving everything else behind.

The first thing I did was to see how Jessie and Tim were doing. They were pretty broken up over the events of that day. After all, Brad was the only dad that they had ever really known. They had become very attached to Brad, hated to see him go and didn't understand why this had happened. I wished I could explain it to them, but I didn't understand it myself. Heck, I didn't even have the chance to say good-bye to him.

I sat with my arms around Jessie and Tim for some time. I didn't even go in and talk with mom; it was important that I stay by my siblings. Mom didn't come to talk to me, either; she stayed in the kitchen. I could feel my anger growing as I sat there while Jessie and Tim cried. I still had not shed a tear and was bound and determined to stay strong. I could not let anyone see how much this had also hurt me.

Mom yelled out that supper was ready and we begrudgingly went into the kitchen. As we sat at the table I could tell that mom was not in a good mood, but I decided to ask her some questions anyway. I didn't care what kind of mood she was in; I felt that she owed us some kind of explanation.

I asked her why Brad had gone and her reply was, "Because I asked him to leave." She said it in a rather defiant, self-serving tone and glared at me with her black eyes. Whenever she looked at me in that fashion, I could just feel the hate and anger she had inside of her.

I asked her why she asked him to leave and she blew up at me. Her face turned red, she was spewing all sorts of stuff out of her mouth, in that high-pitched tone, and I decided to leave the table and go up to my room. Before I did, though, I grabbed Jessie and Tim to join me. I did not have anything to say to my mother. In fact, I didn't even want to look at her.

On our way up to my room, I was shaking my head in disbelief. I could not imagine why my mother would have asked Brad to leave. That night was a long one. I refused to leave my room and didn't until after mom went to bed. She usually retired pretty early, around 8:30 or 9:00, and as soon as I heard her settle in, I ran back downstairs.

Jessie had fallen asleep in my bed, Tim was in Jessie's bed, and I wanted to make a phone call.

Our only phone was in the kitchen and I rushed to go and call Grandma Baker. She answered within a couple of rings and I asked her if she knew what had happened. She said she did and was silent. I asked her if she knew why it happened and she confessed that she had no idea and gave me her golden words of wisdom, once again: "Just ignore it." Before heading back upstairs I decided to call Lisa and chat with her for a while. She had a way of always making me feel better.

~

With Brad out of the house, things became very strained between my mother and me. In fact, our whole life became strained. Our only income was county assistance, and it was never enough to pay the bills. We had many challenges trying to make ends meet. Mom was not adept at budgeting, so from the moment Brad left I was responsible for getting the bills paid. Mom didn't understand the process and simply left it for me to take care of. Because I wasn't old enough to drive, mom would taxi me around to the local companies to run the payments in, write the checks, or work out payment plans. I always dreaded those days.

We were always behind on our utility and phone bills. The lady behind the counter would give me a look of sympathy when I came in with the bill and a partial payment. I hated, and still strongly dislike, that look of sympathy. I don't feel there is anything more degrading to my soul than sympathy from others. I don't mind empathy; I just don't want people to feel sorry for me.

Thankfully, utility companies cannot shut off service in the winter. Without that rule, I am sure we would have had our power and heat cut off a time or two. We had a big old house to heat and those bills certainly added up. There were also many months when we were in danger of losing our phone. It would just infuriate me when mom would not go in and talk to these people. Thankfully, when we were really behind, Grandpa Baker would go in with me.

Another event I dreaded was going to the grocery store. We received food stamps once a month, and that was our time to stock up on as many things as we could. Of course, being a 14 year old, I didn't understand the concept of coupons, buying generic or how to shop economically. I bought food that we three kids wanted to eat. Naturally, one of the cashiers at the store in town was a mom of one of my friends and I would grin sheepishly as I handed over the food stamps. That was so damaging to my pride that I can still recall the feeling of shame, deep in my gut, that I felt using those things. We didn't have gas money to drive to a grocery store out of town, so this was our only option.

I quit all of my after-school activities. I had no choice. I either had to be home watching over Jessie and Tim, or working. I found a job in a local café as a dishwasher, and the money I made went toward paying our bills. (As I write this, it strikes me that my mother became virtually nonexistent, in a "motherly" way. She simply became another person for whom I was responsible.)

In addition, mom was becoming higher maintenance; she was really starting to act rather odd. Every day there was a new challenge to deal with. Early in the mornings, before my alarm went off, I could hear mom down in the kitchen, banging the pots and pans around and yelling to herself about something. It was so loud that even with the radio on I could hear her from upstairs in my bedroom, hear that high-pitched chatter spewing out all the hate she had inside of her as she denounced our father and his family, our stepfather, and anyone else she could think of. She would get talking so fast that most of the time I couldn't even make sense of the words. I just knew she was a very angry woman.

I wish I could say that this was an occasional event, but it wasn't. It was a daily ritual for me to avoid the kitchen for as long as I could before going off to school. By the time I got in the kitchen my patience was stretched paper-thin. I would walk in, grab my cereal and juice and sit at the table. Before long, Jessie and Tim would join me.

I am not sure if mom even noticed when we came in there. She would be standing at the stove, in her nightgown and robe, with the same blue curlers in her hair, frying eggs for her breakfast and rambling away on some tangent. I would look up at her with disgust and tell her to shut up and stop talking to herself. Of course, I knew that would only make it worse—and it did.

She would glare at me with fury in her eyes and deny talking to herself. True to form, I wouldn't let it drop until she finally became furious with me. I would usually end the argument by leaving to go to school, but only after it had escalated to the point where she'd howl at me about what a rotten, miserable kid I was.

I dreaded coming home after school. One afternoon in November 1981, I walked into the front porch, through the door and saw pictures of my mom's first wedding displayed throughout the house. There were graduation pictures and senior class pictures of her and our father set up on the dining room table.

This confused me. As I was growing up, I had gotten the belt if I ever asked anything about dad or wanted to see photos. Now, they were displayed around the house as if he were back in our lives. I was stunned as I walked around and tried to figure out what was going on. I asked mom about them and she turned on me, shrieking about how things had not turned out the way she had expected.

Each day my mother and I ended up fighting about something. Her temper would turn on a dime, especially towards Tim and me. We reminded her of my dad's side of the family, and she would take it out on us for any little reason. She liked to take the fly swatter after Timmy.

One time that I recall that happening, she was about to hit Tim with the metal end of the swatter and I had had enough and stood between them. She tried to get around me to hit him and I hit her first, with my hand. She pulled my hair so hard that my head fell back and I grabbed on to her hair the same way. I was not going to let her continue to hurt Tim just because of who he was.

Within moments, she stared at me savagely and said, "If it wasn't for you damn kids, I would be married and living with my doctor right now." I could not believe what she had just said to me.

We let go of one another's hair and I asked her what she was talking about. She said that she had been waiting for her doctor to come and get her, so they could be married and live together. She went on to tell us that if it wasn't for us kids he already would have come and knocked on her door to take her away. Apparently, she felt he didn't want to be saddled with children.

I was shocked by the words I had just heard come out of my mother's mouth. I took Jessie and Tim upstairs, came back down and called grandpa and grandma. They were just across town and I was hoping one of them would come over and talk to mom. I told grandma what was going on and as always, she told me to just ignore it.

I tried to reach Nathan, but I didn't even know where to call him. When I did find a phone listing with his name, there was no answer. I went back up to my room and we consoled each other the only way we knew how, by sticking together.

As time went on we continued to hear about mom's fantasy of her doctor coming to get her. She assured us that, when that time came, she was not going to take us with her. It reached a point where I tried to never leave my siblings home alone with her, but sometimes it couldn't be helped. I had to work as many hours as I could, because we needed the money.

I finally figured out that mom asked Brad to leave because she thought she was going to marry one of her doctors. She would tell us quite often how she expected her "knight in shining armor" to come and take care of her. She was waiting expectantly for that to happen. Mom was sure that if a man with money would marry her, she would be happy—and she sure didn't want us kids to prevent that. You see, mom had decided she wanted more out of life than what Brad could give her; once again, things hadn't turned out the way she expected them to.

Mom's days were spent sitting at the kitchen table, drinking coffee and talking to herself. It was one of the longest winters I remember enduring in my entire life. It was a lot to handle on my own.

I became an angry, bitter and rebellious teenager. I hated life, I hated my hometown and, awash in all that hatred I virtually destroyed the one true friendship that I had. I started to hang out with the wrong crowd and let my friendship with Lisa die. I stopped calling her; I wouldn't return her calls or stop by her house in the mornings before school.

I didn't know what was happening to me. I started drinking a lot, and sneaking out of my home late at night on the weekends, and coming home in the early morning hours, usually about 4:00 A.M. or so. Mom had no clue this was happening. My new friends and I would drive around on the country roads at night and drink until we got sloppy drunk. It became a matter of routine for me to drink a quart of straight vodka, whiskey, or blackberry brandy. No mixing in soda for me. I found the harder it was, the better I liked it.

Chapter Six

In the spring of 1982 things were really deteriorating. Jessica could not fall asleep unless she crawled into bed with me, and Tim usually ended up sleeping in Jessie's bed. Mom was taking more and more Tylenol every day.

Mom had a lot of aches and pains, but she couldn't go to the doctor as often anymore because we did not have the money to pay for the gas to get her there. Come to think of it, we did not have money for anything. It was awful. Some months we couldn't even afford to buy toilet paper, or Kleenex, or paper towels. We had to resort to using the weekly shopper newspaper that we got for free, for our hygiene needs. I was doing the best I could with what we had, and yet it was never enough.

About then, my home economics class took a field trip to the local fabric store. I had never been in there before, even though it was right on Main Street in town. We took the bus down to the store, and within five minutes I was crying and walking back to school with a couple of friends in tow.

When I walked into the store, I saw this elderly lady smiling at me. I didn't know who she was; I figured she was just being friendly, so, though I really wasn't in the mood, I gave her a half-smile back.

She walked over to me and said "Hello Peggy." I looked at her and suddenly realized it was my father's mother—my Grandma Dean! I realized this was the lady that my mom always chased out of our home. Instantly, I broke down in tears and had to leave. I tried to stop crying but I couldn't. My only solution was to get out of there.

I said nothing further, ran out the door and stood there on the side-walk. Kim and Jenny, a couple of friends, came out to check on me with the teacher. I had no idea Grandma Dean worked there, and I couldn't deal with the emotions I felt at seeing her. I was terribly embarrassed by my crying, yet I couldn't control it.

My teacher asked me what happened and I couldn't even tell her. I just said, "I can't go back in there." I pleaded for her to let me return to school and she agreed on one condition: I couldn't go alone. That was fine with me and both Kim and Jenny joined me for the long walk back to school.

In hindsight, I wish I had talked to my grandmother that day. Maybe she could have helped us kids somehow, or put us in contact with our father or something. I was just plain scared when I saw her. I had been told all these bad things about my father's family, and the only thing I felt I could do was walk out.

I hadn't cried for a long time, and I don't know why the emotion was so overwhelming that day. I imagine it really hurt her when I left. She looked so happy to see me, but I just could not handle it. She didn't know what was going on in our lives. I am confident if she had, she would have done something to help. In fact, I know she would have. Realistically, I don't believe outside of my mom's family anyone really knew what was going on at our home, and I sure didn't make it a practice to tell anyone.

In May of that year, I came home one day and found that mom had taken an entire bottle of Tylenol while we were in school. Mom was taking more and more pills all of the time, but this was ridiculous. She was delirious and half-dazed, and I asked her what had happened. She showed me the bottle of pills and said she had emptied it out while we were at school.

I called my grandparents and they came and took her to the hospital. She was admitted into the Stress Center, and we were told we could go and visit her in about a week. It was decided by Grandpa and Grandma Baker, and Edith and Bob, that we kids would stay at home and take care of ourselves until we received some information about mom's condition. That turned into a three-month adventure.

When school was out I did what I could to earn extra money. Besides working at the café, I mowed lawns and babysat any chance I could. My grandparents checked in on us regularly but most of their time was consumed by taking care of mom. We never saw anything of our older brother. In fact, I hadn't seen or heard from him since the day that he came and told us that Brad was leaving. It was at that point in my life that I told myself that I didn't ever want to end up in a situation like my mother. I believe, even today, that that is a motivating force for me.

During that period, I found that getting drunk on the weekends was not enough anymore. I also discovered that I could take my mom's car out for a drive and not get caught. I didn't have my license or permit yet—I was still only 15—but that didn't matter; it was a way to get around.

Mom had a green Buick, from when she and Brad were married. It didn't have any insurance on it, because we couldn't afford it, so it hadn't been driven much. I found when I took it out that it did have quite a bit of power under the hood. I became pretty destructive. I would take it out, pick up my friends, and drive—way too fast— around the town and the roads that surrounded it.

We would drive over to the liquor store in Hemlock to buy booze. I looked the oldest and was always the one who had to go in and do the purchasing. (The owner *had* to know I was under-age; thank goodness the laws are much more strict today.) My group included two boys and two other girls. We didn't date each other at all, we just hung out together. To be included in my group you had to have a bad attitude and a questionable home life, and you had to like to drink. These people fit the bill just fine.

For excitement, I would try to break into the local swimming pool at night. I never did make it in, but I sure had fun trying. Sometimes, when my other friends were not available I would take Tim and his buddies out with me to drive around or create havoc wherever I could.

I was getting an unfavorable reputation in town. Some nights, the police sat outside my house waiting to see where I was off to that evening. When a policeman did show up, I would sneak out the back door after Tim and Jessie were asleep, and I thought it was pretty cool that a cop was waiting for me and didn't catch me.

My world was a horrible mess, yet I don't even think I knew how bad it was. I was simply in survival mode. I became pretty withdrawn. I gained weight and didn't care what I looked like; my cousins would complain to grandma that at family events I would just sit there and not say anything or be any fun.

Grandma being the person she is, felt compelled to share with me what my cousins thought and what they were saying, and she wanted to know why I was that way. This interrogation would infuriate me, but I would never reply. After all, what did they expect from me? To be a happy and carefree teenage girl? How could they even think that that was a possibility? What did I have to smile about? I had no control over my surroundings, my life or the events that were taking place in it, and everything had fallen apart around me.

In August of 1983, just before school started, mom's doctors had decided that she needed longer term care than the Stress Center could give her. Her mental health was not improving, and a stress center is only a short-term solution for people who experience nervous breakdowns. Our mom needed long-term treatment, so she was committed to a state hospital for the mentally disabled. She would not be allowed to come home for quite a while. The news did not really surprise me, yet I was concerned about what this meant for Jessica, Tim and me.

Obviously, we could not go on living alone. My grandparents and aunt and uncle were trying to figure something out. My siblings and I wanted to stay together, but that was not an option. Who was going to take in three teenage kids? They decided to split us up. We would live with different family members, but the fact that we'd be with kinfolk didn't help the situation much.

Our unspoken pact of always being there for each other was being violated. This was the hardest thing that any of us had endured up to this point. I had always told Tim and Jessie that I would never leave them and that I would always be there for them. And, now, we were being separated.

They were going to a town about 50 miles south of me and would be with different families, but within several blocks of each other. The day they left was an excruciatingly painful day. It absolutely broke my heart. We were so much more than just brother and sisters. They had been my responsibility for so long that I suppose it was similar to having your own children taken away. Over the years, we learned to rely only on each other; and now that was gone. I don't believe I have ever felt so alone in my entire life. I will always remember that August day that I had to say good-bye to the remaining pieces of my family, and yet remain strong.

The plan was for me to live with my grandparents so I could stay in my hometown and finish high school. I was entering my junior year, had just turned 16, and couldn't care less about anything.

Up until then, I had managed to remain a pretty good student. That year, my grades faltered, I started to skip classes when I could, and I became known as quite the partier. Some days, I was still drunk when I went to school in the morning. Other days, my friends and I would dare ourselves to drink in class. We took little sample bottles of booze into our math classroom and sat in the back and took swigs when the teacher had his back turned.

I started to lie to my grandparents about my whereabouts and would sneak into our old house whenever the chance arose, and I would still take mom's car out for a spin now and then. I had taken my permit test, although I still did not have my license. We had an early freeze that year, which created perfect conditions for winter driving contests in the school parking lot. I would meet my cousin Kenny there and we would see who could do the best 360 in the car. I kept going until he conceded that I had won.

My friend Kim and I had this great plan to have a party in the structure (house) I still considered to be my home. Even though we weren't living there, our furniture and things were still there. I told my grandparents that I was staying overnight at Kim's home and she told her parents she was staying overnight at mine.

We had planned on just having a little party at my home. Well, anyone who has tried this knows that it gets out of control—fast. Word spreads that there's a party at a certain location, and *everyone* shows up. My house was full of people. There was a fire on the kitchen stove caused by somebody trying to cook something. Guys were playing hockey on the kitchen floor. There were people everywhere, even upstairs in the closets and bedrooms. Mom's Christmas decorations were destroyed by people trampling on them in the closets.

I was drunk and I left. What a stupid thing to do—leave your own party. I had to go for a booze run. I remember that when I got back, I just stood in the street staring at all the lights on in the two-story home and could not believe what was happening. I walked in and people were telling me how great my party was and that it would go down in history as one of the all-time favorites. As I walked through my house, I could see that this party was completely out of control. I grabbed a couple of my friends and asked them to help me kick people out. We didn't have much success until it was between midnight and 1:00 A.M.—curfew time for most kids.

Kim and I spent the night there, and the next morning the telephone rang. The neighbors had seen, and heard, all the commotion at the house and they called grandma that morning. I had this bad feeling as I picked up the phone. I wasn't supposed to be there, and by picking up the phone I was admitting that I was.

Sure enough, it was grandma, and needless to say, she was pretty upset. She said, in a flustered tone of voice, "Peggy, you have lied to us one too many times and we are through. We are just through with you, Peggy. We're done." And she hung up. I looked at Kim and told her what had just happened rather nonchalantly. I don't think the phone call did much to me emotionally except to fuel my "I don't care" attitude.

Within an hour grandpa stopped over to make sure that we were getting out of the house and to deliver the clothes that I had had at their home. He looked sad, though he was just following orders. The furnace had gone out, and he was making sure that it was back up and running so the pipes wouldn't freeze. He asked where I was going to go and I said I wasn't sure. He didn't reply.

I really had no idea what to do; I was 16 years old and homeless. We called Kim's parents, explained the situation and asked if I could stay there for a few days. They agreed—while reminding Kim that she was now grounded for quite some time.

I gathered some clothes, took the Buick and Kim and went out to her house. (I am sure grandpa must have known that I had the car and yet, today, I am wondering why he allowed this.) Kim's family didn't have much money, nor did they have much room in their home, and we knew this was a short-term arrangement. Her parents had agreed to allow me to stay there for at least a week.

That following Monday in school I was quite the celebrity. Everyone was talking about what a great party I'd had. It was said it would go down in history as one of the best my class could remember. I didn't find much support for the outcome of that party, however. I ended up shuttling back and forth between Kim and Jenny's house for the next several weeks. I am thankful their parents agreed to the arrangement.

By November of that year the living arrangements were reaching the end of the line. A more permanent arrangement was needed, for all of us. I just didn't know what that would be. I hadn't spoken to my grandparents since that fateful day after the party.

Part Two

A Lost Soul

Chapter Seven

One evening, during a week I was spending at Kim's, I received a phone call. One of my distant cousins, Kelly, had decided that she and her family would like to take me in. They were in the same town as Tim and Jessie and told me they wanted to offer a helping hand. She and her husband, Butch, had decided that I couldn't go on living week by week in different homes and thought this was a good solution. Besides, it would get me closer to my brother and sister.

It was actually Butch who called me and I believe he had had to do a persuasive sales job to get Kelly to approve of this arrangement. They had been told that I was a no-good, rotten teenager and that they would be idiots to take me in, yet they decided to anyway. They had a two-year-old girl at home and didn't have much room in their little house, and yet they decided that they would try it for a while and see what would happen.

Butch asked me if I was interested. I told him I would have to think about it and hung up. I looked at Kim and didn't know what to do. We went into her room, which we were sharing, and discussed it. I didn't want to leave my hometown, and yet we both knew that it couldn't go on like this. We both sat and cried when I decided it was my only real option. Kim had become a friend to me like Lisa had been and I hated the thought of losing her.

Butch came to get me, and once again I packed my things, jumped in his truck and hit the road to a new home. I was very apprehensive as we drove away from Meadowbrook, but I reminded myself that at least I would be near Jessie and Tim again.

Kelly and Butch's home was very small; only two bedrooms, and the baby (Michelle) had one of them. They put a cot for me in Michelle's room until further arrangements could be made. They laid some ground rules, got me situated in my new school and graciously accepted me into their home.

Even though it was my junior year of high school, I still didn't have my driver's license; fortunately I had some friends that did. Initially, one of my friends from Meadowbrook would come over and get me most weekends, picking me up right after school on Friday and bringing me back on Sunday afternoon. As time went on, those trips became fewer and farther between, either because I was grounded for something, or I had to be at home to baby-sit Michelle, or just simply because the friendships were drifting apart.

That winter, Butch built a room for me downstairs, in the basement, and it was great to have my own space. I was slowly, but surely, adapting to my new life. I was glad to be back in the same area as Jessie and Tim, and we spent as much time together as we could. School was OK, but it was difficult to come into a new school in my junior year. It was another small school, with a junior class of about 75 students or so, and it was another case of everyone knowing everyone else and everything about them.

Being a new girl, I got some attention from the boys. Any time there is a new girl in a school that small, she will attract attention. Unfortunately, some of the girls didn't like the attention I got, and that started things off on the wrong foot. Partly as a consequence, I pretty much tried to hang onto my life in Meadowbrook as long as I could. I didn't get involved in any activities in my new school; I just went home and helped out where I could with the baby and the house. Kelly worked part-time, usually evening hours, at a local grocery store and Butch worked varying shifts at a factory.

That spring I got my driver's license and whenever Butch let me take the truck, I headed over to parties in Meadowbrook. Hanging around with my old friends, I would drink as much I used to. Things had changed, though, because I was out of the loop. Kim and Jenny each had boyfriends now, but I still hadn't really had a boyfriend myself. Sure, when I was drinking I would occasionally make out with someone, but it never developed into anything more than that. I didn't have much interest or much confidence in my ability to attract a guy.

I would get drunk at the parties and then hop in the truck and hit the road for that hour-long drive home. I am very lucky that I never killed anyone, or myself, by doing this. I don't know how I did it.

One night, though, as I was driving home wasted from drinking a quart of whiskey, straight, with some of it spilled on my shirt, I was pulled over by a cop. I was one block from home when the cop's lights and sirens went on.

I had been speeding through town, going 55 in a 30 mph zone, and he caught me. He walked up to the window, I rolled it down to talk to him, and I couldn't even sit up straight. I was virtually leaning against the door as I handed him my license.

He looked at it, looked at me, and gave me a citation to get the exhaust fixed on the truck. The muffler had been missing for some time and the cop had been on Butch's case to get it fixed. It was pretty loud and the people around town didn't like it. When I woke up the next morning I couldn't recall if I had only dreamt about being stopped, or if it had really happened

Whenever I had been out late at night partying, Butch made sure to wake me up early the next day on some pretext. It was his way of teaching me a lesson. This Saturday morning was no exception. He came down and knocked on the door to wake me up at around 7:00 A.M. and said we had to go do some work out at his folks' farm. I groaned as I crawled out of bed—I had a monstrous headache—and groaned even louder when I saw the ticket on my dresser from the night before.

I was afraid to tell Kelly and Butch, and yet I had to. It was his truck and he needed to know about the required repairs. I think I was grounded for a while, although, it didn't matter much due to the fact that I didn't have much of a social life in my new town anyway. I did have a job at the roller-skating rink, and between that and babysitting Michelle, I was kept pretty busy.

My siblings and I would get together most days after school, but things had changed between us. I think so many things had happened to us that it was impossible to regain the closeness we'd had, but we sure tried. Soon after I got my license I bought my first car for $100. It was a big, old, green, two-door Chevrolet Impala that did not have any side rear windows. Butch took me to check it out, and he gave it his approval. I was so proud the day I drove it home. It didn't matter that it was a load of junk and louder than heck, it was my own car.

Our school was about five miles from home, and now that I had a car I picked up Jessica and Tim each morning. We cherished those trips in my car. We drove down the highway, with the music as loud as it would go and the three of us sang along as obnoxiously as we could. It did get quite cold in that car without the back windows, but it didn't matter. The three of us would pile into the front seat and have a "good old time."

As I said, I like to drive fast and my self-imposed challenge each morning was to leave home after the bus left and to arrive at school before it did. I would race down the road and, as we approached the bus, the kids could hear me coming down the road, (thanks to the blown muffler), and they would wave at us as we sped by. It gave me a thrill to go blowing by that school bus.

Chapter Eight

My relationship with Kelly and Butch was unique. Kelly and I tolerated each other; we were two very different people. She had been the Dairy Princess her junior year, had beautiful blond hair and blue eyes and had always been a "good" girl. She and Butch were High School sweethearts and had married within a year after graduation. Kelly was happy being a mom and wife and living within three blocks of her parents.

Butch, on the other hand, became my friend. His family life had not been as "ideal" as Kelly's, and he could relate to some of my experiences. He was a tried and true country boy with blond hair, blue eyes and known for being a hard worker. He seemed to take a real interest in helping me deal with the things that had taken place in my life. Many times over, he would take me on walks around town and drives around the countryside so that we could just talk.

It took me some time before I could open up to him, but eventually I did. I didn't trust many people and had developed a pretty hard shell around my heart, but Butch seemed to really care about my well-being. It was rather nice; I hadn't received that kind of interest from anyone since I was a little girl hanging out with my dad, and Butch did become a surrogate father to me.

I shared with him all the things I was feeling and told him how unhappy and confused I was about life. I went to him with my problems and he was a good listener. In fact, he was the only adult in my life who didn't think I was worthless.

Butch got into the practice of taking my hands and holding them while I was talking, or putting his arm around me. Initially, I resisted all such attempts, but he persisted until I gave in. He would tell me to trust him and that he was just doing it to help me get through some things in my life.

Within a few months I gave in, and yet it still felt uncomfortable. But I stopped backing off or moving away or grabbing my hand back. In many ways I was very naïve. As I look back on that situation, I know I should have seen the writing on the wall, but I didn't. I chose to view his actions as fatherly affection and support and refused to think anything else of it.

When summer hit us with its barely tolerable combination of stifling heat and humidity, I sometimes chose to sleep at night in the nude. I had a door on my room in the basement, and I was the only one down there and didn't think anything of it. One morning, however, while we were all eating breakfast together, Butch commented on the fact that I hadn't worn much to bed the night before.

I looked at him, as red and embarrassed as I could be, and didn't know what to say. Kelly was sitting right there and laughed at his comment and I just chose to ignore it. I didn't know enough to ask how he knew that, and I was neither confident enough to make an issue about it nor intelligent enough to stand up for myself. As soon as I was done eating, I jumped in my car and hit the road for a drive. I reminded myself that I was lucky to have a place to call home for a while and that I had better just leave well enough alone.

Of course, it didn't stop there. One evening I was babysitting Michelle because Kelly was at work. It was about 8:30 or so; Michelle had been put to bed and I was watching television in the living room. Butch, who had finished up early at his job, came home and was going to freshen up in the bathroom. Before he did that he was fiddling with the mirror that was on the hallway door directly across from the bathroom, and I didn't pay much attention. (Keep in mind, that the house was very small; it had two bedrooms, a living room, a kitchen and a bath on the main level. From wherever you stood in that house, you could see the entire living area.)

Well, the next thing I knew the mirror was facing my direction and Butch was standing naked in the bathroom touching himself. I had never seen a naked man or his "unit," and I didn't know what to do. I was rather disgusted and immediately went down to my bedroom. That night I wished that my door had a lock on it, but it didn't. I put a chair up against the door to block it and stayed in the room until Butch left the house the next morning for work.

He never did come down those steps, and I am sure glad I didn't have to find out what else was on his mind that evening. I was rather quiet the next morning, but Kelly didn't seem to notice. She didn't know me well enough to read my moods, and I wasn't about to say anything to her about the events of the prior evening.

As soon as I saw Jessie and Tim later that day, I told them what had happened; none of us knew what to do about it. I figured that if I just ignored it, it would go away. I was not in good enough standing with any of my relatives to tell them about it, so the three of us just decided to let it go.

The relationship between Butch and me was definitely strained for some time after that night; neither one of us said anything to the other about it. I started to say no to his invitations for walks, drives, or doing anything with him alone. Sometimes, though, being alone together in the house couldn't be avoided and on those occasions I just kept my guard up and stuck to myself.

Chapter Nine

That Spring, 1984, I attended the Prom in Meadowbrook and was also asked to attend the local one by a neighbor boy, Danny. I decided to go because I couldn't say no to him. He was nice, though I didn't have any feelings beyond friendship for him. This would be the first event I had attended at my new school. I had been there about four months and nobody knew anything about me. Well, Prom changed all of that.

We went to the dance and out to the bonfire afterwards. I drank a little and had fun talking with my classmates. Danny ended up going home without me because I was having too much fun with the group of people who were out there. I felt bad about it; I didn't want to hurt Danny, but I was having fun and didn't want to leave. Poor guy, didn't even get a kiss out of his prom date.

From then on, my friends in Meadowbrook became part of my past. I had a new group of friends and I found myself getting back into my old habits. I thought I had rid myself of that time in my life, yet here I went again. I started skipping classes and hanging out with the "wrong" crowd. I didn't feel I had a chance to mix with the "good" kids because we didn't have much in common.

I basically hung out with the kids who liked to party. I was not drinking as much as I had been over in Meadowbrook, but I still did my fair share. There was one big change, though: I didn't drink hard liquor any longer. I think I had burned myself out on the stuff in my younger years.

One afternoon I was at a party out in the country somewhere with my friends Bud and Hank. I hung out with a lot of men in my youth and, I guess I still hang out with a lot of men as an adult. Must be the tomboy in me or something? Anyway, the three of us had had quite a bit to drink, and Hank ended up getting in a fight with his girlfriend, who had arrived with some other friends.

Their argument turned into a heated yelling match and concluded when Hank decided to leave. He jumped in his truck, motioned for Bud and me to get in and sped off just as we had gotten the passenger door closed. Even though he was quite drunk, I still climbed in the truck with him.

We were on a narrow, curved gravel road and Hank was driving way too fast. I kept telling him to slow down, but he wouldn't listen to me. I was holding on to the dash as best as I could, but I was still sliding into either Bud or Hank throughout the curves.

Well, Hank hit one curve way too fast and we crashed. The curve came up rather suddenly, Hank tried to turn fast enough to make the corner and we ended up going straight off the road, flying in the air and doing two end-to-end flips before we stopped. The thing that made us stop was a tree.

It is really a miracle that all three of us walked away from that accident with nothing but bruises. We weren't wearing seat belts, and I have no idea how we survived that crash. When we landed, the only casualty seemed to be my missing glasses; within moments, we found them—like us, intact—in the cab of the truck.

It was a frightening experience and I know I did not take it very seriously. In fact, none of us did. A friend who had been driving behind us saw the whole thing happen, and I think he was more shaken up than we were.

I never did see any cops come around from that accident. I am not sure how we got out of there without any authorities being alerted, but we did. The truck was towed by someone Hank knew, and, with that completed, we found a ride back to the party. By the time we arrived, news had spread of the accident and we were the center of attention for the rest of the day.

I obviously did not have much respect for my life then or really care if it continued or not. Why would I have been dumb enough to jump in a truck with a drunk, angry man? How could I go back to the party as if nothing happened? There had to have been someone, up in Heaven, watching out for me; otherwise, I am confident my destructive patterns would have gotten the best of me.

The next life-altering event that took place was the death of Butch's mother. It happened rather unexpectedly; she was at work, went to use the restroom, and had a heart attack. Butch was concerned about his father being out on the farm by himself, and within two weeks after the funeral, we were packing up our belongings and moving to the country. We were moving in with his dad.

It was a big old farm house that didn't have a duct system to get heat, or air, upstairs to the bedrooms. Butch's dad had the only bedroom on the main floor; the rest of us were upstairs, and it got mighty cold up there during the winter and miserably hot in the summer!

Due to a company lay-off, Butch lost his job and was at home all of the time. Kelly tried to pick up more hours to help out with money; they did receive a monthly check for taking me in and I know that helped out considerably.

Slowly, but surely, I began to trust Butch again. Time has a way of healing wounds, and he hadn't made any further advances since that evening. Once again, I considered him my friend. I think I just wanted someone in my world to be a father figure, and he was the person most available. It is amazing how we will overlook personalities or situations when we just want everything to be OK.

Butch and his father had very similar personalities, and they clashed quite often while we lived there. Within a year of moving to the farm home, we were packing up our things and moving again. This time, it was just down the road. Kelly and Butch had bought a neighboring farm that allowed them to raise cattle and a small crop. They needed help with chores, bailing hay, cleaning the barn and watching the kids. By this time a little boy had been added to the family, and I wanted to do as much as I could to assist the people who had taken me in.

I liked the way Butch listened to me and believed in me. I had never experienced that before. However, he also made me nervous at times because of the way he looked at me or acted. There were only two bedrooms in the house, both upstairs, and neither of them had a door. The room I shared with Michelle was directly across the hall from Kelly and Butch's bedroom. The baby slept with them in their room.

Kelly and Butch had hung a sheet over their doorway to allow themselves some privacy. Nevertheless, they had a pretty active sex life and I could not help but hear them. I hated lying in my bed listening to those two go at it. I would stay up as long as possible before I went up to my room each night. Often I would fall asleep only to be awakened a few hours later by the sounds of their activities. To make matters worse, the following day Butch would invariably make some comment about what had taken place the night before. He always got such a kick out of seeing how embarrassed I got when he talked about his sex life. It actually disgusted me more than embarrassed me.

~~~

My senior year of high school went well, comparatively speaking. I could not wait to graduate from high school. I really had no idea of what I was going to do with my life, but I knew I wanted to do something great with it. I hadn't an inkling of how to make that happen. In May of 1985 I graduated and felt like I had my whole life ahead of me. I looked at my diploma as a sign of freedom.

Chapter Ten

That fall I packed up my things, hit the road and headed to Fairview. I was going to attend school at the Vo-Tech to learn bookkeeping. A friend of mine from Meadowbrook, Susan, was attending the college in Fairview, and we decided to become roommates. We rented an apartment that was actually the top half of an older home. The people who lived on the lower level were a young family with one child and it worked out great. Our entrance was in the back, and we did not have to enter "their" part of the house to get upstairs.

One week before moving out of Kelly and Butch's house, I turned 18. Kelly took me out for a drink. The legal drinking age at that time was 18, so we went out to celebrate my becoming an adult and moving on with the rest of my life. She took me to see the Chippendale dancers. They just happened to be in town and she thought it would be fun for me to see something like that. I had no objections to going and watching good-looking men dance around. I was kind of nervous about it, and yet it sounded like it would be fun.

We got home around midnight and Butch was still awake. He had the kids in bed and he was up watching television. Kelly was tired and went straight up to bed, but I was too wound up to sleep and decided to sit up with Butch and watch television. He was rather curious as to what I thought of the "dancers" and quizzed me extensively. I didn't respond much; I basically tried to ignore his questions.

In the middle of some late-night movie watching Butch said he was going to head up to bed. "Fine," I said; I was actually looking forward to having some down time on my own. Before he headed up, though, he came over and sat on me—straddled his legs over the chair I was sitting in and attempted to grab my breasts and kiss me.

I panicked and pushed him away with all my might, and ran up to my room. I was so angry that I laid awake the entire night. I was just infuriated by what had happened. I wondered why my life never seemed to go smoothly for very long. I asked myself why Butch would do this to me and how I should react. Do I make a case out of this, or just leave well enough alone?

Within my family I had always been given a label that was not positive, and I had just finally started to regain some of their respect. Grandma Baker and I were on speaking terms again and had achieved a level of mutual understanding, Kelly and I had finally created a bit of a relationship between us, and I had gotten to the point where I felt I could completely trust Butch again. Now, this happened.

Butch woke up early, as usual, to go and do the chores. Kelly was up with the kids, and I got up, ate breakfast and left before Butch came back in. It was around 8:00 A.M. as I jumped in my car and hit the gravel roads with a strong determination to make things right in my life.

I was going to see my cousin Josh, the one that Jessie lived with. He is Kelly's older brother, and I felt if anyone would listen to me it would be him. We had always had a pretty good relationship, and he seemed to be the most understanding and open-hearted of any of my relatives.

Josh and his wife Mary were rather surprised to see me so early in the morning. Jessie was still sleeping, and as I came in and stood in their kitchen they could tell that something was troubling me. I stood silently for several moments before I had the nerve to say anything at all. Once I started, though, it just came gushing out. I told them about the exposure a year prior, the lewd remarks and the crude approach that Butch had made a few hours earlier.

They looked at me and seemed as surprised as I was initially. I was thankful they didn't question me about what I'd told them and I felt immediate relief at sharing the news. We decided that the best thing to do would be for me to go and talk to Kelly about it. We decided that Josh would join me for moral support.

As we left Josh's home we were both pretty nervous. Neither of us wanted to tell Kelly about her husband's advances but, what else could we do? I drove my car back out to the farm and Josh followed me in his truck. We wanted to arrive and meet with Kelly before Butch had finished his chores and were back out at the house by 9:00 A.M.

When Kelly saw us come in together she asked what was going on. When I left I had told her I was going in to see Jessie and Tim and to not expect me home for some time, yet here I was, back within an hour, with Josh.

Kelly was sitting in the living room folding clothes. Her children were playing on the floor beside her. I sat on the couch directly opposite her and Josh stood beside me. I think he was too nervous to sit down.

Neither of us knew how to start this conversation, so we were making small talk. Kelly is one of those people who always has a smile on her face and I hated to tell her what her husband had done. But I had to do it. I took a deep breath and started to repeat to her what I had told Josh. My voice was shaky, my palms were sweaty, and my stomach was in knots. When I was done, Josh joined in by saying it had been his recommendation that I come and tell her. It was nice to have that support.

I don't know how I expected Kelly to react; in fact, she seemed to take this news in stride. It didn't seem like it was a big issue to her, and yet she said she would talk to Butch about it and make sure that he apologized.

Josh thought that was great and asked me how I felt about it, and I said it was fine. I didn't know exactly what I was looking for by telling Kelly about Butch's behavior, except for the fact that I didn't want it to happen again. I was willing to forgive and forget and move on.

As Josh left to return home, I felt an immense sense of dread. With him gone, it was pretty uncomfortable being there, and I decided to leave again. I didn't have any plans other than to get out of there. Kelly asked me to be back in time for lunch, noon sharp, and to help out with things around the house that afternoon. As I jumped in my car and hit the gravel roads, I had no idea what to expect when I returned for lunch.

I ended up back in town hanging out with Tim and Jessica. When I told them what had just happened, they were about as angry as I was, but none of us knew what the solution was. All I could keep thinking was that I was glad that I would be moving out within a few days to start my own life.

That morning seemed to drag; I was not really looking forward to lunch. Once again, as I pulled into the driveway and got out of my car,

I had that upset stomach and those sweaty palms. I had no idea how I was supposed to react when I entered the house with Butch and Kelly casually getting ready for lunch.

Sure enough, as I walked in the back door, Butch was already sitting at the table helping to feed the kids. Kelly was getting the last items ready, and she asked me to grab the milk before I sat down. I did what was asked, sat down at about the same time Kelly did, went through the ritual of saying grace, and started my meal without looking at Butch. I didn't have the courage to look his way, and I avoided all eye contact.

I chose to stay silent while the usual small talk was going on about the weather, the crops or whatever. Before long, Kelly said, "Peggy, Butch has something to say to you." He cleared his throat, looked at me and said, "Pig-Pig (my nickname) I am sorry for what happened last night."

I sat there, looked at him and didn't respond. Kelly suggested that I accept the apology and I begrudgingly did. Immediately after that, Kelly was back to her normal, smiling self, talking about the kids and the things to do that afternoon.

As I finished eating and cleared my plate, I began to feel strongly that I needed some of my own space. I could not believe that the apology was the only action that would be taken, and that the incident already seemed to be forgotten. As I headed upstairs to my room, I felt my inner anger surging, but I had no idea what to do about it.

I kept thinking that maybe there was something wrong with me that caused me to take this more seriously than they did; maybe I was just over-reacting to what was just an honest mistake on Butch's part. However, while Kelly was down getting the kids cleaned up, Butch came upstairs.

I had been lying on my bed, and, as soon as I heard him heading up the steps, I jumped up and stood by the edge of the room, which was at the top of the stairs. He came within a few feet of me and said, "Pig-Pig, the only reason you told on me is because you liked what I did to you. You feel guilty about that and wanted to cover your tracks." With that, he turned around and headed back down the steps and out the door to the barn.

I felt like I hated him—both him and Kelly—and went and lay back on my bed and cried. What was I to do now? Make more of a scene, or just let it go?

Because I felt that I had no other recourse, I decided to bide my time. I couldn't get into my apartment until the first of the month, but that was only five days away. Until then, I would be gone as much as possible, help out where it was expected, and then move on with my life. I didn't feel that this was a battle worth fighting.

It did really hurt, though. I was 18 and had way too many experiences under my belt. Butch was someone who had been important to me and he had betrayed me: I felt sure he must have been scheming from the very beginning to try to seduce me. At first he had seemed so sincere about helping me, yet the moment I became a legal adult, he tried to force himself on me.

It had taken me a long time to learn to trust anyone, and the person I had decided to trust turned out to be unworthy. I felt stupid and angry, and violated, and my "who gives a damn" attitude came surging back. It had disappeared for the past year, and it came back now, roaring like a lion.

That final week in their house was one of the longest ones of my life. I kept to myself, did what I had to do and left it at that. I was counting the hours before I moved out.

Chapter Eleven

As I was moving into my apartment, I felt as though I had a new lease on life. I was excited to be on my own and creating a new world for myself. It was nice to be back with Susan and getting to know her again. There were some adjustments that had to be made, as there are with any roommate, but we got them figured out and really enjoyed living together.

I spent most of my time at school or at work. I was hired by a restaurant and worked as many hours as I could while maintaining my school schedule. Initially, I was pretty serious about doing well at school and found it rather enjoyable.

At work, I met a girl named Sabrina. She was my age and we hit it off immediately. We had so much fun together while we were at work that we started to hang out together after hours. She had two jobs and was not going to school. We pretty much became inseparable.

She had worked there longer than I had and was part of a group of people who went out together regularly. I was accepted into that group immediately, and most of our nights were spent at one bar or another. It was a good time.

I was back to drinking pretty heavily again. It wasn't hard liquor, as it had been in high school, but I still knew how to drink. The more partying I did, the less serious I was about school. Still, I maintained a B average while attending fewer and fewer classes.

Life was bringing me down. That fall my mother had been released from the hospital, spent about a month in a half-way home and was given an OK to live on her own. Grandpa and Grandma Baker bought her a trailer home, in Deerborne. That is where all her doctors and her contacts at the human resource center were, and there was a "Trac" bus system that could get her around town.

By state law, Jessie and Tim had to go back and live with her. They had just begun to feel settled in their new homes, and they had to move again. It was awful knowing that this was not the best thing for them. But she was their mother.

Jessie and Tim were happy about this arrangement in some ways, but in other ways they were not. On the bright side, they would be back together again, and they knew that mom wouldn't impose too many rules on them. At the ages of 16 and 14, that seems like a pretty good deal.

However, I started getting lots of phone calls from them, asking for help. I was always the person my family relied on to fix things. It is rather ironic, isn't it? I was the one with the "label," yet I was the one who was always expected to take care of situations that arose. I got calls from Grandma Baker, mom, Tim and Jessie on a daily basis and found myself running to Deerborne a couple of times a week to straighten things out for them or to take care of something with mom.

After the Christmas break I quit school. My hours at the restaurant had been increasing to the point where I was working full time because I needed the money. I found that I liked hanging out with my friends more than going to school and decided that was the route for me to go. I don't know what I was thinking; probably, I *wasn't* thinking.

In February 1986 I was packing up my things and moving again. Sue had a boyfriend who she was going to live with and I could not afford to stay in the apartment on my own. I found a room to rent from a single mom on the edge of town. As I was packing my things, and then unpacking them again, I wondered if my life would ever settle down.

I started drinking heavily again. I felt at a loss. I was so messed up. So many things had happened and I couldn't make sense of any of it. Sabrina was on the road much of the time, training employees for new restaurants that were opening. I worked in the kitchen preparing food for the buffet line. I thought about entering management, but I couldn't deal with the politics to get me there. I had a pretty large chip on my shoulder, made painfully obvious by an attitude that said, "I can do things on my own and I don't need help from anyone." How wrong I was.

~

There was lots of pressure building from my siblings, and I didn't know how to help them anymore. Hell, I couldn't help myself; how was I going to make their lives better? I couldn't help the fact that they had to live with mom. I felt awful about that, but what could I do to resolve it? I went over there when I could, and I offered support by always being available by telephone.

I know it was not easy for them to live with mom. She still talked to herself constantly and was very moody, especially when I was there. There was still a lot of hate built up within her and we still ended up fighting quite often. Many times, when I stopped by to see Tim and Jessie, I wouldn't even talk to mom. It was just better that way.

Life seemed so unfair. I was unbelievably angry, but I had no idea how to channel that anger or to work through it. In time, I decided the best thing for me to do was to leave Minnesota and everything that life had brought me. I decided I had to get away from all the people who had hurt me, all the experiences that were painful, and all of my mistakes. I was completely fed up with every aspect of my life. Everywhere I turned there was another heartbreaking experience, and I thought that my only options were to stay and continue down the path I had been following or to start another one. I chose the latter.

One Sunday morning in May I got up early and went and bought a paper at the gas station just around the corner from where I lived. I was scouring the want-ads for anything that looked like it would help me get out of southern Minnesota.

Within moments I found an ad about an opportunity to live and work in Vail, CO. The first couple of lines sounded intriguing. I had always dreamed of seeing Colorado and the scenic beauty it supposedly offered.

At the bottom of the advertisement I saw that the ad came from McDonald's. They were hiring people out there and even supplied a place to live. I dreaded the thought of working for McDonald's. I had spent my entire working life in restaurants, but I had never gone the fast-food route because I had never wanted to endure that kind of work-day. At this point, however, working at McDonald's seemed to be the least of my worries.

I was pretty nervous as I dialed the number out in Vail. It would have been around 7:00 A.M. there, and by a stroke of luck the manager, Terry, was available to talk for a few minutes. She seemed really great and supplied all of the information I needed to make my decision.

Terry said that McDonald's had leases at a few different rental complexes throughout the city, where six to eight employees would live together in one duplex. Rent and utilities were taken right out of the paychecks. Jobs were available, and she suggested I send in a resume for her to review. I thanked her for her time and hung up.

As I hung up that phone, I already had made my decision: I was moving to Colorado! I did not want to take the time to send in a resume; after all, it was only McDonald's, so how hard could it be to get hired to work there?

That Sunday was a busy day for me, because my objective was to be on the road that night. Once I had decided to do this, I didn't want to sit around and think about it; I just wanted to leave. I was tremendously excited about this adventure, which I felt was going to fulfill my quest for happiness in my life.

I was supposed to work that day; I called my boss, Tom, and quit with no notice whatsoever. He was surprised to hear of my plans, but he wished me well. I spent the rest of the day running around and packing up what little bit I owned. I had a Ford Escort and knew that I could not take very much with me—just my clothes and some keepsake items that I had.

I didn't own much furniture, and what I did have I just left in the house that I had been living in. I took some extra boxes over to mom's house that afternoon. I didn't mind running over there because I wanted to tell Jessie and Tim, in person, what I was doing. As I was driving down the highway, to Deerborne, I was trying to figure out how to present this to them without feeling that I was abandoning them. I didn't really care if mom knew or not; it was just important to me that my brother and sister understood why I was doing this.

Mom was surprised to see me and was even more surprised when she found out about my plans. I was so proud of myself as I shared the news that I was moving away. I felt it was about time I did something for myself instead of for everyone else around me.

Telling Jessie and Tim was not as easy. Some of their friends happened to be there, and I suppose that forced us to control our emotions somewhat, but I could tell they were not really happy with me. Oh, they were excited for me, but knew what it meant for them: they would be living in Dearborne without me to call on. It meant that I wouldn't be around to deal with the challenges that came up or to provide a shoulder to lean on. It meant that I was leaving them behind. We hugged and shed a few tears before I headed out the door.

My mind was just racing as I jumped back into my car and hit Highway 2 heading back to Fairview. I had a ton of things to get done, and the first one was to buy a map and figure out how to get to Vail, Colorado.

That day was one of anticipation. My spirits had not been so high in years. It just felt so great to be doing something with my life. Even if it was going to work at McDonald's, I felt it was a step in the right direction. It never even crossed my mind that a job would not be available for me when I got there.

By 10:00 P.M. I was ready to head out for my new adventure. The only other people I had called that day to inform of my move were Sabrina and Grandma Baker. Sabrina was excited for me; she knew what I had been going through and wished me well.

Grandma was a bit more subdued. She was stunned when I told her of my plans and even more so when I said I was leaving that night. She was worried about my traveling alone, that far, with no previous experience for such a thing. She was worried about my living 18 hours away. She was worried about me because, after all, she is my grandma and she was the one who virtually raised me. As we said good-bye, I promised to call her when I arrived at my destination.

I did a final walk through the house to make sure I hadn't forgotten anything and then left. As I got settled in my car I was scared to death. I think the reality of what was taking place finally hit me. I had never been beyond the borders of southern Minnesota as an adult. Heck, I had never even driven through a major metropolitan area.

Yes, I was scared; nevertheless, I felt there was no turning back. I just had to go through with what I had set out to do. I started my car, took a deep breath and hit the road.

Chapter Twelve

The further I got from home the better I felt. Sometimes, being naïve about a situation, and just plunging forward, is better than looking at all of the "what-ifs" that could lay ahead. I only had $100 to my name, but at that point in my life $100 was a lot of money, and I was sure it would be enough to get me by until my next paycheck.

I stopped to get some sleep at a rest stop in Nebraska, along Interstate 80. It was around 4:00 A.M. and I just couldn't stay awake any longer. I had rolled the windows down, had the music blaring and was drinking lots of high-caffeine pop, still my eyes were dropping. I thought nothing of pulling my car into that parking lot, locking the doors, leaning my seat back and going to sleep. I shudder at that thought of doing that today.

Within a couple of hours the sun was coming up and I was back on the highway. As I crossed the state line into Colorado, I let out a yelp of excitement. Nebraska had been flat and boring, and, to my amazement, the eastern side of Colorado wasn't that pretty either. But I had never seen a real live ranch before and was excited at each new discovery that I made.

I reached Denver just in time for the evening rush hour. It was about 4:00 P.M. and I had never seen so much traffic in my life. I panicked for a moment, then gathered my wits by simply taking a deep breath and driving slowly. There were six lanes of traffic in each direction, and I had no idea where my turn-off was. I was trying to read the map and just could not do it while navigating my way through Denver. I ended up just throwing my map in the back seat, working my way over to right lane and hoping and praying that a road sign would point me in the right direction. Sure enough, there was an exit sign that said Vail, and I was on my way.

It's about a two-hour drive from Denver to Vail, and it was one of the most beautiful stretches of highway that I had ever seen. Of course, I had grown up surrounded by flat farmland, and I was now immersed in mountains and trees. In every direction I looked the scenery was just gorgeous. I was straining out my window to try and see everything that I could and had to remind myself to pay attention to the road.

Driving through mountains was a learning experience. I couldn't figure out why my car was slowing down so much. I was putting the pedal to the floor and I kept going slower and slower and slower. Cars were passing me, honking their horns and I was getting more flustered because I didn't know what was happening to my vehicle.

Finally, it dawned on me to downshift to a lower gear to gain more power for moving up this mountain. I let out a huge sigh of relief as I shifted into fourth, and sometimes third, gear and was able to go faster. Once I figured that out, the rest of the trip went smoothly. I'd only had a couple of hours of sleep, yet I didn't feel tired at all. I was filled with excitement and anticipation for my new life.

As I entered the town of Vail I was awestruck by its beauty. I had never seen anything like it! The town is nestled in a valley of the Rocky Mountains. The sun was working its way to the west and everything was so plush and green. The landscaping, along the highway and throughout town, was beautiful with the spring flowers in full bloom. Everywhere my eyes gazed it was clean and prestigious. At that point, I didn't know that Vail was an upper-class ski village. One of my first hints was when I saw a policeman drive by in a Saab; they sure didn't have vehicles like that back home.

My first task on arrival was to find the McDonald's, get hired and find a place to sleep. Terry was not there when I arrived. She didn't know I was coming because I hadn't told her; one of the assistant managers, Matt, called her on her mobile phone and asked her to come to the store.

I grabbed a bite of food, filled out an application and waited for Terry to arrive. As I was sitting in the booth I started to realize how tired I was and fought to keep my eyes open. Luckily, Terry wasn't too far away and within an hour I was an employee and getting back into my car to find my new place to live.

The roads were winding and steep, but Terry had given me a good map. It was an odd feeling when I went and knocked on the door to meet my new roommates. We were not separated by gender, and I was put wherever there was a vacancy. I ended up in a place with seven other people, male and female, who were from different areas of the country and who had come out here for pretty much the same reason I had: to run away from life.

After I was settled, I walked out onto the deck to watch the sunset; it was awe-inspiring. I was standing in a valley of mountains stretching to see everything within eyesight and felt a little homesick as I stood there by myself and shed a tear for the people I had left behind, mainly Tim and Jessie.

Within moments I pulled myself together and decided I should let people in Minnesota know that I had made it here alive and well. I called Grandma Baker, Sabrina and mom, and they were all relieved to hear that I was safe and settled in.

I was accepted immediately into my new world. I worked with, lived with, and hung out with the same people. We were all in the same boat; none of us had any money, and we were separated from family and friends. Needless to say, we all became pretty good friends; we were all we had.

Vail was a very expensive town, and we couldn't afford to take part in any of its activities, but it was fun to drive around and watch people and dream of what life could be like. I had never seen so much extravagance in my life and was in awe of people with money.

Inside myself, however, I was kind of numb towards everything. I was not ready to face anything that I had run away from and just wanted to live for the moment. I was pretty quiet and didn't share anything about my past with anyone. I was starting over and wanted to forget what I had left behind.

Matt, whom I met when I first walked into McDonald's, ended up being interested in me. I had heard numerous times, from various people, that he wanted to go out with me; initially, I wasn't interested.

He was nice enough, and he treated me with respect. He was in good shape because he ran every day, was about four years older than I was and had white complexion with red hair. But I simply was not interested in having any type of relationship, with anyone, at this point in my life.

He was persistent, though, and I finally gave in. Who knows what compelled me to finally agree to go out with him? It could have been loneliness, the circumstances that we were all in or my just not wanting to disappoint anyone. He wasn't really my type, but we started hanging out together more and more. He seemed to be getting pretty serious about me and I was basically indifferent. He was coming off a major heartbreak that had spurred him to move to Vail, and I think he was looking for someone to fill that void. I happened to be there at the time.

As far as I was concerned, we were more friends than anything. He showed me pictures of his ex-love and told me how much she had hurt him. He had been truly devastated by their break-up and was looking for someone to share his life with.

I, too, had been devastated by what life had done to me, but refused to share much about myself, my dreams or my past. I felt that neither Matt, nor anyone else, would accept me if they really knew what my life had been like, and besides, I was not ready to face up to it yet.

After living in Vail for three months, I found myself packing my belongings into my Escort and getting ready to hit the freeway, again. This time, though, I was heading further west, to Oregon.

By that time Matt had been in Vail for one year, and that was all the time he had allowed himself for this "phase" in his life. He had kind of floundered through life thus far, and it was time for him to get some things figured out.

Matt had grown up in California; his folks had moved to Oregon after he left home to go to college. His mother, Faith, grew up in a privileged San Francisco family. His father, Jim, had grown up as a Navy brat and had lived all over the country. Matt was one of three kids; with twin sisters who were younger than he was.

Matt's parents had high hopes for him, and I don't know if he ever met their expectations. He was accepted into West Point for college but ended up quitting. I believe that he went there to make other people happy, didn't really know what he wanted to do with his life, and subsequently found out he wasn't ready for the lifestyle of West Point.

Matt was heading to Oregon and had asked me to join him. This meant we would be living together, and even though I wasn't really sure how I felt about that, I found myself agreeing to go with him. I didn't want to hurt him by turning him down, but I was apprehensive about my decision.

He knew that I did not reciprocate his feelings, yet he somehow accepted it. I didn't have anything to stay in Vail for. It was too expensive to really enjoy doing anything, I didn't, relish, my job and my attitude about this move was that I had nothing to lose by going for it. I didn't think about what the future would bring or what my decision meant. I was simply in survival mode.

We each had a car, and we decided to drive both to Oregon. There were two women who were driving back to Washington together at the same time, and we decided to kind of travel as a group.

~

We had very little money as we headed out on Interstate 70, but that didn't phase me. I had been poor all of my life and was not deterred by the fact that we were traveling with virtually nothing but gas money.

It was wonderful to see the countryside of that part of America. We traveled through Utah and Nevada before reaching the state line of Oregon, but we did not drive straight through as I had when I moved to Vail. We spent one night sleeping in a rest stop and the second night sleeping out in the desert air. It got colder than I would ever have imagined in the desert that night.

We were pretty good about keeping together. With three vehicles it can be a challenge to follow one another, so we would set certain meeting points or just naturally stop if one of us got too far ahead of the others. It was usually I who had to stop and wait for the group to catch up. I did this once in Utah somewhere; it was just a little town, the kind that if you blinked you would miss it.

The road that I had been on was winding around and around; I had seen only a few homes scattered along the hillside. Then I saw a little business area along the highway. I saw a gas station and decided that this would be a good stop. I could fill up my tank, use the restroom and wait for my group.

As soon as I pulled up to the gas pump, opened my car door and got out, I swear that every person in the general vicinity came to the doorway of his or her place of business or home and stood there, straining to see who I was. Within moments there were maybe 20 people staring at me inquisitively. Not one of them smiled at me or said hello. They just stood and stared.

This was one of the first times I actually felt scared. I decided to pass on filling up my gas tank or using the restroom. I quickly got back into my car, locked the doors and waited for Matt and the others to show up. Not one of those people moved or did anything threatening, but they stood there glaring at me for about 20 minutes, until the rest of the group arrived. It was one of the longest 20 minutes of my life.

I was thrilled and relieved when people I recognized drove up behind me. Once the townspeople saw that there was a man in our group, they all went back inside to resume whatever it was that they had been doing. I was flustered as I shared my experience with Matt and couldn't wait to drive away from that town. I don't think I sped ahead much the rest of the trip; I had learned my lesson and decided to stick pretty close to the people that I was traveling with.

Chapter Thirteen

We arrived at our destination within three days of leaving Vail. We drove right to Faith and Jim's house, wished the two women a safe trip as they headed on to Washington, and proceeded indoors to start over again.

Thankfully, Faith and Jim were still at work and this gave me some time to gather my wits about me. I was feeling rather confused about lots of things. I was trying to be as happy about this arrangement as Matt was, but I just couldn't be. I didn't want to hurt him by any means. He really wanted to have a relationship, and I was the willing party at the time. I didn't want to disappoint anyone else in my life. I was tired of doing that.

I was really nervous when Faith and Jim arrived home, but I needn't have been; they graciously accepted me into their life. We ended up living with them until we found jobs and saved up enough money to find a place of our own to rent and make the appropriate deposits.

Matt found work at a Texaco Station on the outskirts of Eugene, and I found work at Izzy's Pizza Restaurant in Springfield. The two cities border each other and are distinctly different. Eugene is a white collar, well-educated community, whereas Springfield is more of a blue collar community where the lifestyle is reminiscent of the 60's.

While we were still living at Faith and Jim's, I was awakened one morning with the news that my car was gone. Jim had first noticed it. He was heading out the door to go to work around 7:00 A.M. and saw that my car was not parked in its usual spot by the curb. He looked around the block to see if I had parked it elsewhere and didn't see it. He came running back inside, hurried down the hallway to our bedroom, knocked loudly on the door and yelled, "Peggy, your car is gone."

Both Matt and I jumped out of bed and ran outside to see for ourselves. Sure enough, my Escort was nowhere to be found. We all thought someone had stolen it and I immediately called the police.

It turned out it had been repossessed. As I hung up the phone, I was dumb-founded. I didn't say a word and just walked back in to our bedroom. Matt followed me back there while Faith and Jim were asking rather excitedly what I had found out.

I hadn't been able to make a full car payment for quite a while. In fact, I hadn't made any payments during the three months that I was in Vail. However, I had sent, just recently, a check for $50 with an explanation of what was happening. It was too late, though. The bank wanted the car back.

I was terribly embarrassed that this happened. Matt's folks had no idea that I was behind on payments or that we were struggling financially, at least, not to the degree that we were. When I told Matt what had happened, he went out to tell his folks. They were astonished, and hurt, by the fact that we hadn't told them how far behind I was on the payments before this happened.

I was at a loss about what to do. I didn't have the money to get it back, nor did Matt, I was not going to take money from his parents. The conclusion Matt and I reached was that we would just have to get by with his truck. We would have to drive each other to work and back, or make arrangements with co-workers.

It was a liberating day when we finally had enough money to rent an apartment. It was challenging living with Faith and Jim. That says nothing against them; it was purely me and my discomfort with the entire situation that made living with them uncomfortable.

The next thing I knew, Matt wanted to get married. I was not ready for that. He knew how I felt about "us," but he wouldn't give up. At one point I agreed to marry him just so he would leave me alone.

He was absolutely thrilled with my decision; I wasn't. Immediately after I said "yes" I felt strangled. I just couldn't go through with it, and within a month I told him so. I had tried to talk myself into it and convince myself that this was a good thing to do, but, in fact, I simply wasn't in love with him. Sure, I cared for him, but I did not feel the kind of love that says "I want to spend the rest of my life with you."

When I shared my feelings with Matt I could see the disappointment on his face. The hurt he was feeling shone through and I felt absolutely terrible. What was wrong with me? Here was a person who genuinely cared for me, would do anything to bring me happiness, had helped support me for about six months, and I could not love him. I tried and I just couldn't make it happen. At the end of our conversation we decided to stay together in the hope that, in time, my feelings would change.

Work was going pretty well. I worked any chance I could get, anywhere they could use me. Washing dishes, preparing food, dealing with customers at the front counter—it didn't' matter to me. I just wanted to work as much overtime as I could. Rent was expensive, neither of us was making much more than minimum wage, and we had to save some money to buy me a car.

The only friends I had were the people I worked with. We did nothing socially outside of work, yet they became pretty good friends of mine. They all knew what was going on with Matt, and I knew about their love lives.

Before long, I had an opportunity to go into management and, naturally, I killed it with my attitude. I still carried that "chip" on my shoulder that showed I didn't know how to play the politics in any business structure.

I kept in touch with my family back home by calling them as often as I could. I would check in with Grandma Baker when I had something to share that she would be proud of. I didn't call her very often, but when I did she sounded happy to hear from me. Other than that minimal communication, I enjoyed being detached from the problems back home. It still amazes me, though, that I failed to see how I was creating problems of my own.

Chapter Fourteen

In May 1987, at the age of 19, I found myself married and pregnant. I now know that my son is one of the greatest gifts I have ever received in my life, but, at the time I found out I was pregnant, I was not thrilled. I had left Minnesota because I was tired of caring for other people and now I was going to be a mom. I certainly had not accomplished my original objective.

Matt and I were married in Reno, Nevada and I had a feeling of dread that day that I couldn't shake. An unwelcome thought kept forcing its way into my conscious mind and that thought was: "Peggy, what on earth are you doing?"

My gut told me this was the wrong thing to do. I had thought marriage was supposed to be a commitment people made only if they were in love with each other, but here, once again, I was functioning in survival mode. I didn't feel as if I had any options.

Matt was ecstatic that I had finally agreed to marry him. Faith and Jim were pleased and eager to have me become part of their family. My grandparents were thrilled that I was taking this step. After all, their definition of success and happiness for a woman was that she be married and have a family. Everyone around me was happy with the decision I had made.

Everyone except me. Far from sharing their happiness and excitement, I felt trapped and completely helpless. Nevertheless, I was determined to make the best of the situation. I thought if I tried hard enough, I could find a way to be happy in my life with Matt.

In July of that year, things were getting worse at home in Minnesota. I started to receive more and more calls from Jessica and Tim about the problems they were having. Tim had failed his previous year of school; both he and Jessie were behaving as I had during my last few years of high school, and, to top that, mom had tried to commit suicide again. They desperately needed help. I felt that the only solution was for me to go back there and do what I could to help. I talked to Matt, and he agreed to move to Minnesota that following month.

We quit our jobs, packed up our belongings, said good-bye to Matt's family and headed out of town, once again following one another down the freeway. With two old vehicles and almost no money, we drove to Minnesota on a wing and a prayer.

Neither of our vehicles was in very good condition. I had bought a used Subaru shortly after we moved into our own apartment. It wasn't a car anyone who wasn't pretty desperate would want to drive across the country, but it made it. Matt drove his little truck while pulling a small hand-made trailer filled with our furniture. Our vehicles were packed so tightly that we barely had room to sit in the driver's seat of each one.

We had a few problems on the way home. I had a flat tire before we got out of Oregon. It happened on the east side of Oregon, in the desert area of the state. Thankfully, it was still light out when it happened and there was a shoulder for me to pull onto. I drove the rest of the trip on a spare tire.

It was slow going through the mountains of Idaho and Montana. We had to be careful to not overheat either my car or Matt's truck. I don't remember noticing the beauty of this drive or the scenic areas we passed through. I was focused on one thing and one thing only: making it to Minnesota. I was not thrilled to be moving back; it was an obligation. I also thought that with a baby on the way it would be nice to be living near my family. Yet, I don't recall feeling any inner excitement or joy about this trip. I just recall the anxiety I felt virtually every minute of the four days it took us to get there.

As we were driving through the plains of South Dakota, Matt hit a deer. It was dusk and he never saw it coming across the freeway. I was driving behind him and saw it jump up out of roadside ditch. I wanted to try to warn Matt but I didn't have time; it happened so fast that I didn't even have time to honk my horn. When I saw the deer bound out of the ditch, it was inevitable that Matt was going to hit it.

What a bummer! There we were, sitting in the middle of Interstate 90, with the front end of Matt's truck ruined and the radiator spewing out coolant. There were no other vehicles in sight, no one to ask for help, so I drove to the nearest town where I found a repair shop with a tow truck. I locked up my car, jumped into the tow truck with the driver and went to get Matt and his truck.

We could not go another mile without having some repairs done. The dent was probably going to be permanent, but we had to get the radiator fixed. Our next challenge was finding money for the repairs. We didn't have any credit cards or extra money; our only option was to call Faith and Jim and ask for help. They wired us some money and we waited about a day for the repairs to be completed. We couldn't afford to stay in a hotel, so we slept in a nearby rest stop, off the freeway, and returned to town the next day to wait.

Thankfully, the rest of the trip was uneventful. When we arrived in Deerborne, we drove right to the trailer park where mom, Tim and Jessie lived. They were home waiting for us to arrive, and as soon as they saw us pull in they ran out of the trailer to meet us.

None of them had ever met Matt before, and were thrilled to finally be meeting their brother-and-son-in-law. It was good to see mom and great to see Jessica and Tim. They looked a little rough and yet, at that moment I realized how much I had missed them. I had been gone for a little more than a year, and a lot had taken place in all of our lives since I had left.

Even though mom's place only had two bedrooms, we stayed there for about a week. We just slept on the living room floor, leaving most of our things packed in our vehicles.

It only took me an afternoon to find a job—after all, my job search was pretty limited. The only thing I had ever done was work in a restaurant, so the obvious places to start applying were the pizza joints right there in Deerborne. There were three of them and I was hired at the first place I went, Godfather's Pizza.

When I went to fill out the application, the manager interviewed me on the spot. I did not tell him that I was pregnant. I wasn't really showing yet, and I had worn some baggy clothes. I wore sweats to the restaurant and explained that we had just moved into town and hadn't unpacked yet. That was true, but it was really just an excuse because nothing but my sweats fit me at this point.

I was afraid that I wouldn't get the job if I told him I was going to be having a baby that winter. I had not even thought about how I would handle the situation when it became obvious that I was pregnant. All that mattered to me then was that I needed a job. I was hired for the 8:00 A.M. to 3:00 P.M. shift. My role included the prep work for the day and working through the lunch rush, wherever I was needed. It is amazing what people will do, or say, when they are just simply trying to survive.

Shortly thereafter we found a place to rent. It was an old house that had been built in the early 1900's. It was a white, 1½ story house with a one-car detached garage. It had a front porch, an open, winding staircase to the upper level, a living room, a dining room, a small television room, and a kitchen with lots of windows along the outside wall. The two bedrooms were upstairs and the hardwood floors throughout the home were gorgeous. We went to lots of garage sales to find furniture for our new home.

Jessica and Tim began to spend all of their time at our house. They virtually moved in without actually bringing their clothing or beds over. While it added stress to my life, it was actually kind of nice to be with them again. We had always had fun together. I stepped right back into the role of caring for them—and my mom.

I don't recall experiencing any of the joys of pregnancy that I had heard about and had seen in other people. Some women just glow and are so thrilled they can hardly wait for their bundle of joy to show up. I disliked every moment of pregnancy. At the time, I thought it was just because I didn't want to get fat. In retrospect, I now realize that I hated pregnancy because I was unhappy with the situation I was in. I had left home looking for freedom, and I hadn't found it. I was back in the same situation that I had tried to leave behind, but with added responsibilities.

In addition to his full-time job, Matt took on a part—time job, on the weekends, in a little convenience store just down the block from our house. My due date was February 25, 1988 and we had to save as much money as we could. In fact, I worked right up until the weekend that I had the baby.

On Friday morning, February 26, I was having light contractions and decided to go to work anyway. The contractions remained light throughout the weekend, but by Sunday evening they were coming closer together. The big moment had arrived, and it was time to go to the hospital.

The hospital that my doctor was registered with was about 45 minutes away from Deerborne. Our son was born at 2:10 A.M. on Monday, February 29, a leap-year baby. He was a precious little thing, and the whole idea of motherhood scared me out of my wits. I don't recall any inner joy from giving birth, or any excitement about being a mother. All I could think was, "What am I going to do now?"

We made calls to our families, and Tim, who had been up all night wondering what was going on, was so excited that I'd had a boy he couldn't even sleep. Matt was ecstatic, and his parents were thrilled that there would be a son to carry on the family name.

Labor was hard on me. My face was swollen and blood vessels popped in my eyes from pushing so hard. I looked as if someone had beaten me with a baseball bat. Jeremy was only a little over five pounds at birth, but he had been developing inside of me in an unusual, u-shaped position.

His legs had been hyper-extended so that his feet were up by his face, and when he was trying to come out, his feet would stop him. We hadn't had an ultrasound done, and the doctor had thought that I was going to deliver a rather large baby. It turned out that Jer was not very large, it just felt like he was because of his position.

When he finally came out, his legs popped right back up to his head. It was odd to see and it scared me a little bit. He had to wear a brace for the first three months of his life, to keep his legs down. The brace made him look like a frog, but it forced his legs to stay down and bent. Every time we changed a diaper, we had to take off that brace and then replace it when we were done.

We were home within a couple of days and doing fine. Like any new parents, we found bringing the baby home for the first time to be frightening and almost overwhelming. Just figuring out what the different cries mean can be trying.

Chapter Fifteen

Luckily, Jeremy was a very good baby. Tim, Jessica and I thoroughly enjoyed playing with him. He had precious blue eyes, reddish/orange hair, and the chubbiest cheeks and belly around. I loved him from the moment I laid my eyes on him.

As much as I loved my baby, however, within four weeks of bringing him home I went back to work. We needed the money, and being at home all day was driving me stir-crazy. I was going crazy because I had a lot of time to think about my life and how unhappy I was. It didn't even dawn on me that I could have used that time much more productively in many ways, such as getting involved in the community, or finding some books to read to enrich my mind and soul, or simply creating a warm, loving home for my son to grow up in. I didn't want to face the facts of my life, and I thought if I went back to work and simply ignored my unhappiness, things would take care of themselves.

I had an opportunity to get into management training later that spring and I went for it. I started working lots of nights and weekends. Matt and I rarely saw each, but our working opposite hours meant daycare was not an issue.

In May 1988 Jeremy was baptized and Matt's family made the trip to Minnesota for the ceremony. We had just bought a car, a used but nevertheless sporty Datsun Z28, that we had to show off to them. It appeared that everything was going well for us; on the outside.

By the first of July that year, I knew that I couldn't stay with Matt any longer. I couldn't keep pretending that our marriage was a good thing. I couldn't keep pretending that I was happy. I had no idea what I wanted out of life, I had always gone from one bad situation to another throughout my life, and felt I just could not go on with this anymore.

It got to the point where I couldn't even stand the thought of kissing Matt, let alone having an intimate relationship with him. I now realize that he wasn't the problem; I was. But at that time I knew only that I was back to feeling trapped again. I was back to being a mom for Jessica and Tim and for all practical purposes being a mom to my mom. I was married to someone who loved me but whose love I did not reciprocate, and I was now a mother to a sweet little boy. I was absolutely miserable and I didn't know what to do about it.

So, I did what came naturally to me, what I had always done: I ran away. I had been doing quite well in management and was offered an opportunity to manage a Godfather's pizza about 45 minutes southwest of our home. This gave me an "out," a reason to run away; it also started me down what would be a long and painful road.

I think Matt had come to realize how unhappy I was so we decided that I would move out on my own, closer to my new restaurant. The plan was for this to be a temporary situation; I would move out and take some time for myself to determine what was important to me.

The most difficult thing I have ever done was to move some of my things out and leave Jeremy behind with Matt when I left to settle in my new apartment. Moving out and saying good-bye to my child tore violently at my heart. It wasn't as if I was never going to see him again, but I was moving out.

When I made the decision to leave, I knew in my heart that at that time I was incapable of being a good parent to my son. I knew he would be better off, at least temporarily, with Matt. Still, I cried bitter and copious tears as I drove away. There were times I was crying so hard I couldn't even see the road. To this day, I can feel the intense pain I experienced as I drove down I-35 away from my son. I was so ashamed of myself. Why couldn't I have just stayed and made it work? Why couldn't I have just been happy with what I had?

I threw myself into my job. I would go home after a long day of work and cry myself to sleep. Many times, when work was slow I would start to cry and lock myself in my tiny corner office. I was miserable, but I didn't have a clue about how to resolve it.

I spent my days off in Deerborne, with Jeremy. I took him to the park and on walks around town, and I sat and held him as much as I could. He was a wonderfully happy, smiley baby and it was very hard to drive away from him when my visits were over. When I did see Matt, we were cordial but our encounters never went beyond just saying hello to one another. Some days, it was just too painful for me to go to see Jeremy. I felt tremendous guilt for my actions, and I found myself avoiding the situation whenever I could.

I heard all sorts of comments and accusations from my family members. That is, from everyone but Tim and Jessica. They still accepted me and stuck by me. My Grandma Baker could not believe what I had done. None of them understood how I could leave my son and in all honesty, I don't really know either.

I just know that the bottom line, for me, was what was the best thing for Jeremy. And at that time Jeremy's best interests lay in staying in his home, with his dad. When I was growing up, I don't believe anyone in my world ever stopped to ask themselves what was best for us kids. It was always what was best for our mother. I was determined not to take that misguided approach with my child. I couldn't take care of myself, how could I take care of him?

That October I had received word from Tim and Jessica that Matt was moving back to Oregon and was going to take Jeremy with him. Matt had not talked to me about this yet he had told them?!

I was furious, but I had no idea what to do. I couldn't blame Matt for wanting to go back home. After all, I had dragged him to Minnesota and then left him. I understood why he would want to be near his own family; neither of us had even tried to talk about reconciliation or our future plans. We hadn't talked about much of anything since the day I moved out.

I didn't know what to do on my behalf. I didn't know if I should go back to him to try and make things work, try to stop him from moving, or just let him go. Who was I to stop him from moving? Who was I to say he couldn't take Jeremy with him? What had I done to show that I deserved to be a parent?

Jeremy was seven months old when I went to spend that last afternoon with him. They were leaving the next morning, and everything from our house had been either packed for Matt to take out west or moved to my apartment.

I walked in through the front porch and saw Jeremy sitting in his swing, as happy as could be. He got a big smile on his face when I walked in, and I started to cry. I didn't want him to see me like that, so I choked back the tears for the rest of the afternoon. We didn't do much that afternoon other than sit and play with each other. He was sitting up really well and I took lots and lots of pictures. I had no idea when I would see him again or what was going to happen from that point forward.

Jessica and Tim stopped by and we spent our time passing Jeremy back and forth among us. I sat achingly and watched the hours tick by. I was feeling more pain than I had ever before felt in my life and I could not believe what was about to happen. I didn't want to let Jeremy go, but I felt I had no options. I wasn't thinking straight or logically about anything. I had never been taught to look at my actions and their implications and take responsibility for them. I had only been taught to ignore challenges, in the hope that they would go away. Well, this didn't seem to be one that I could ignore.

At the end of the visit, I had to virtually drag myself out of our home. I was devastated at the thought of what I was letting happen. I was devastated at the thought of my son, Jeremy, going to live 3,000 miles away from me.

I got in my car, drove to my apartment and cried uncontrollably. Sitting on the floor shaking, and holding myself, and rocking back and forth. I felt as if allowing all of this to happen made me just about the worst person on earth. I felt that I would never be worthy of any happiness or success in my life, and that I would never be worthy of getting Jeremy back into my world.

Chapter Sixteen

I cried for days and ended up quitting my job. I could no longer avoid the fact that I had used this job as an excuse to leave my son. It was too painful to go to work every day realizing what I had allowed to happen. I was absolutely miserable and felt the only way to move on was to leave Godfather's Pizza.

I was once again an outcast to the majority of my family members, and I didn't know where to turn or what to do to improve my life. So, as usual, I moved back into a situation I'd previously run away from, but where I at least felt I belonged. I moved back to Deerborne and into the trailer with mom and Jessica. (By then Tim was living with a friend and his family.)

I found two different jobs, in the hope that working long hours might distract me from my anguish. I also saved as much money as I could to send out to Matt. I figured I had to do something to assist, and, though I couldn't send much, I did send something each month.

My days were spent working at Wal-mart in the early mornings as part of the crew that stocked the shelves, and then working in the afternoons and evenings at a restaurant. When I had time off, I slept or lay in front of the television. I did not allow myself any friendships—I figured no one would like me when they learned what kind of mother I was. I did not allow myself to feel any happiness about anything. I was unhappy in my jobs, but what other options did I have?

Matt and I talked occasionally on the phone. He missed having me in his life, and I missed Jeremy. It was a painful holiday season without my son. I didn't attend any of the annual family gatherings, choosing instead to just stay home and sit in my room. I was trying to avoid dealing with life or with the situations that I had created. I had become numb towards the world and was just biding my time. Life was a struggle.

In January 1989 Matt sent me some pictures of Jeremy—the first photos of him that I had seen since they left in October. I stopped home about 1:00 P.M. after finishing my Wal-mart shift to eat lunch and take a break before I was due at the restaurant at 4:00. I saw an over-sized envelope from Matt in my mail, which mom always stacked on the kitchen table for me.

I suspected what I'd find inside and wasn't sure if I had the nerve to open it. I stood and looked at the envelope for some time before I opened it. I had been trying to work up the strength to look at what was going to be inside and thought I had accomplished that.

I sat down, gently opened the envelope and saw the pictures of my son. I could not believe how he had grown and changed, and how much I missed him at that moment. I started to cry and I couldn't stop. I didn't even have the energy to get up and go back to my room. I just sat at the table and wept.

Mom was, of course, home; she always was. Although we had not been fighting as much as we had in the past, we still hadn't forged much of a relationship. When she saw me crying, she came up to me, put her hand on my shoulder and asked if I was OK. My response was more tears, and I nodded my head up and down as if to say, "Yes, I am OK." Even though no words would come out of my mouth, I knew that she was trying to help me.

Matt and I began talking more frequently on the phone. We had never divorced, and we knew Jeremy needed his mom. Matt was living with his parents in their home. Jeremy was lucky to have Faith and Jim in his world, because they gave him the stability that neither Matt or I could.

Before long, Matt began asking me if I would come back to Oregon and give it another shot. At first, I didn't answer him. As the weeks went by, however, I began to realize how miserable my life was and struggled to make a decision about what to do. I wanted to be involved in my son's life, and I wanted him to have both his parents. I still didn't know if I could be happy with Matt, but I had to do something to change a situation I had helped create.

After some agonized soul-searching Matt and I decided to try again and see if there was some way we could make it work between us. During our separation I had discovered that there is a lot more to marriage and relationships than just being "in love." I felt that the right thing to do was to put my best foot forward (if I had one), and I was completely honest with Matt about my feelings at that time, my confusion about life and my uncertainty as to what I wanted. I believe our eyes were wide open as we ventured into a tentative reconciliation.

Within two weeks after that phone call, Matt and Jeremy came back for a visit. They flew to Minnesota and I was unbelievably nervous as I sat in the Minneapolis-St. Paul airport waiting for them to arrive. I didn't know what to say or how I would react once I saw my son. I felt a combination of dread because I didn't want to feel the pain, excitement that I was trying to conceal because, realistically, I had no idea how Jeremy would react to me, and that old, strangling feeling of being trapped in a situation I didn't want to be in.

The plane arrived, and suddenly there was Matt walking up through the gate, carrying Jeremy, and I felt terrified. What was I going to say? How should I greet Matt? Should I be reserved with Jeremy or greet him lovingly?

When they finally reached me, I greeted Matt with a cordial hello and a quick hug. It was an uncomfortable scene. I stood with my hands in the pockets of my jeans, trying to act cool about all of this. Matt stood there with a big smile on his face and a look of anticipation for our future; he looked about as happy as he did the day I agreed to marry him.

As soon as I laid my eyes on Jeremy I knew I could never leave that little boy again. I smiled at him, and, when he smiled back, I knew that somehow we would be OK. He was so cute and I just couldn't wait any longer to hug him. I asked Matt if I could hold Jeremy and he obliged rather eagerly. I grabbed my son into my arms and held him tightly. I wanted to cry but wouldn't allow myself to. I put on a good front that made it appear that I was handling this just fine, but, inside, I was melting with tears.

I didn't want to leave this spot, but I reluctantly joined Matt on the trek to claim their luggage, and then we headed back home to Deerborne. Mom, Jessica and Tim were waiting anxiously for Jeremy back at the trailer. In fact, they had shown greater excitement about this visit than I had. They couldn't wait to see their nephew/grandson again.

It took a couple of hours to get home, and during the drive both Matt and I were quiet. I was immersed in trying to deal with my emotional state and didn't feel like talking. He was tired from traveling with a baby in tow and just wanted to rest. During that drive, I made a decision that changed my life: I decided that I had to do whatever it took to make our marriage work. Somehow, I had to find a way to love Matt and make a home for our child, regardless of my true inner feelings.

Matt stayed for a week and it ended up being a whirlwind trip. We had plans to make for our future and things to settle from our past. That old numb feeling had returned to me, but I was determined to ignore it. I had Jeremy back in my life and that would have to be enough.

When Matt headed back to Oregon, we decided that Jeremy would stay with me for another week, and then the two of us would fly out and meet him. As it happened, Matt's sister, who was stationed in Hawaii with the Navy, was getting married that month, February 1989.

Naturally, Matt's entire family went for the occasion. In celebration of our reunion Faith and Jim invited me to join them. So, Jeremy and I flew all the way to Hawaii to meet Matt and his family there. We were responsible for the airfare, and they paid for our food and lodging.

The flight was a long one, made longer by a snow storm in Minnesota that delayed our flight. We were on the plane for 12 hours before we finally landed at our destination. Jeremy was remarkable for a small child; he spent the entire trip either entertaining the people around us or sleeping. I am blessed to have such a good-natured child.

When we arrived, Jim was thrilled to see me. He is not a man who holds back his feelings and he was crying tears of joy that I was back in their world. As usual, my inability to be happy rendered me rather stoic. Inside, I desperately wanted to be filled with joy and love that I could share with the world, but was just too frightened to let it out.

Hawaii was all right, although I remained pretty sullen throughout our ten-day stay. The islands were beautiful, the weather was great and yet, I could not have cared less about being there. I was thrilled to be with Jeremy, of course; it was the rest of the situation I was not comfortable with. Not enjoying Hawaii may seem strange— even incredible—but the truth is, external surroundings aren't what brings fulfillment to our lives; rather, it is what is taking place on the inside.

Meanwhile, Matt was beside himself with happiness at having me back in his life. He didn't even really know who I was, yet he felt I was the one for him. Clearly, he imagined me to be someone that I wasn't.

When our vacation ended, I headed to Minnesota to get my things and move back out to Oregon. Matt and Jeremy flew, with Faith and Jim to their home, making plans and anticipating my arrival.

As soon as I had made that decision, I was determined to not look back and just move forward. I spent the entire airplane ride home talking myself into what I was about to do. As soon as I landed, I shifted into high gear and was determined to be on the road to Oregon within one week.

There were countless things to do, which probably was a blessing in that my mind was fully occupied. First I had to alert my family of my plans and quit my jobs. A lot of preparation goes into moving across the country, and this time I didn't want to be packed tightly into my car traveling 3000 miles without any money. Fortunately, I had enough money saved to rent a U-Haul truck with a trailer for my car (which was still that sporty Datsun Z28), but knew that I wouldn't have enough money for lodging. That meant there would be a few more nights spent in rest-stops along the freeway.

I was 21 years old and packing up to hit the road and start over—again. This time Jessica and her friend Connie were going to accompany me. They had never been out west, and this trip gave them a good opportunity to see the countryside and gave me some company along the way. Once we hit Eugene, Oregon they were going to visit for a few days and then return to Minnesota on a Greyhound Bus.

The morning we were set to leave, around the second week of March, Grandma Baker had called to tell me that there were blizzard warnings for South Dakota and to urge me to stay behind for another day or two to let the storm pass. But, though it was reckless, I was determined to leave that day. Heck, I had driven in snowstorms in Minnesota and always had made it through. Besides, I didn't want to spend any more time at home to think about what I was doing. I had made up my mind to go and I was going to go regardless of the weather conditions. Mom wished us a safe trip and watched us drive away.

Sure enough, about seven hours from home, we hit the storm. We were driving on Interstate 90, through South Dakota, when the snow descended upon us as only a blizzard can. The winds were howling, the snow was coming down like a solid white sheet out of the sky, and the temperature plummeted. We were all a little scared because it happened so fast, but I assured the girls that we would get through this with no problems.

The seemingly sensible thing to do was to slow down to about 20 mph and look for an off ramp so that we could get off the freeway and stop somewhere until the storm passed.

However, visibility was so poor that every time we caught sight of an exit sign or an off ramp, it was too late to turn off. We had already passed it. Also, we couldn't tell if there was anyone behind us or in front of us that we might hit or be hit by if I were to turn too quickly or brake suddenly to try to enter one of the ramps. So, we decided it was best to wait until we could see one well ahead. Besides, those U-Haul trucks are not exactly known for great handling, especially when they're pulling a trailer.

The snow was getting worse, visibility had deteriorated even farther, and I was seriously thinking of just stopping in the middle of the road, but that was too dangerous. I tried to pull over onto the shoulder, but I couldn't find it. I decided my only option was to keep going straight ahead as slowly as I could and hope the snow would let up.

By this point, we were thoroughly scared. I had driven through many snowstorms before, but never through anything like this, let alone in a truck pulling a car behind it. The winds were high, the heavily falling snow was coming at us almost horizontally, and it seemed as though conditions were getting worse every mile we went. I didn't know what to do. The three of us were straining to see a spot where I could pull off, and it was becoming excruciatingly frustrating to keep seeing those exit ramps only when it was too late to do anything about it. Jessica and Connie started to cry; my heart was racing and my hands were clenched tightly around that steering wheel. I focused intensely on watching the road in front of me so that I wouldn't hit anyone.

My focusing was to no avail. Without warning, I hit something and came to a complete stop. Although we were only going about 20 mph, I heard a loud crunch as I hit whatever was in front of me. I assumed it was a vehicle, but visibility was so poor I couldn't even tell whether it was a car or a truck from my seat inside the U-Haul. I had been straining to watch the road in front of me, yet I hadn't seen anything until the moment I ran into it. I sat there for a moment trying to determine what to do and decided I should step out of the U-Haul to see what had happened and what kind of damage had been done.

As I opened my door to climb out, we got hit from behind. This was a strong blast of a hit. It threw me sideways, into my sister's lap, and before we knew it our whole truck was moving. My door was still open and I was clinging to Jessica and Connie to make sure that none of us was thrown out. Within seconds, we were being pushed into the other lane of the freeway; then, the movement stopped as quickly as it had started.

I sat up, shut the driver's side door and we started moving again. I am sure we were all screaming at this point. This time we were being turned completely around until we were facing the opposite direction. It happened so fast we had no idea what was going on. We had no seat belts on and were thrown around until we were all on top of each other.

Just as we were untangling ourselves, we were hit again. This time it was a little crash. We just felt a bump, probably to the trailer, and didn't get moved around at all. After that second crash, we had been facing the wrong direction on the freeway with the U-haul truck in one lane and the trailer, with my car, in the other one. It was inevitable that someone else would run into us.

I stayed put this time. I was not going to try and get out of the truck after what had happened before. I had no idea what had taken place, but there was no way I was going to get out on that freeway again.

My truck had stopped running and would not start again. I was trying to get that thing going by turning the key again and again and pumping the pedal, but nothing would work. I needed to get my truck off the road but, it was obviously in pretty bad shape.

Defeated, I sat back in the seat, leaned my head back against the cab and waited. I don't know what I was waiting for, but I had no solutions to the predicament we were in. Jessica and Connie were really upset, and I tried to calm them down, though without much success.

Within a few moments, there was a man by my door, knocking on the window. I rolled it down, hoping that he could help us. He was checking to see if we were all right and I told him that we were. We didn't have any broken bones, just a few bruises; we were more shaken up than anything. He began to walk away and I said, "Hey, wait a minute. What happened out there?"

He told me that the first crash was when I ran into him and his Chevy Blazer, which he had stopped in the middle of the freeway. The second and third hits were from a semi-trailer truck that ran into us. That is what had forced us into the other lane and turned us around. The fourth impact was from a little Volkswagon Rabbit that hit the trailer again.

I was amazed; I'd had no idea what was happening when we were being thrown around. Upon further questioning, we learned that no one had been hurt, but that my Datsun was totaled and the U-Haul was wrecked beyond repair.

The man thought he would be able to repair his Blazer and the Volkswagon had just been dented on the front end. The main concern right now was getting everyone off the freeway. The semi driver put out some emergency flares and called a state trooper on his CB.

It seemed like an eternity before anyone showed up to help us. I know the police got there as soon as they could, yet we felt half-frozen by the time they arrived. All of my winter clothing had been packed into the back of the truck, and none of us had mittens or heavy coats available. It had been warm and sunny when we left home.

We didn't get out of the truck until help arrived. It had been too close a call last time for me to gain the courage to leave the cab I was sitting in. When we saw some flashing lights through the falling snow, we felt a sense of relief. There were two or three police cars, one of the officers came over and told us to go get in his car. We did that with no hesitation.

The three of us sat in the back of his car for some time. We could see, faintly, that cars were backed up along the freeway now; we tried to determine the condition of all the vehicles involved in the crash, but the blizzard was making it virtually impossible to see clearly. We were waiting for the tow trucks to arrive from the nearest town to get all of us, including the semi, off the road. It was the only way my stuff was going to be moving.

When the trooper got back into the car, he gave us a stern welcome. He lectured me, hard, for driving in this kind of weather and stated that I might be getting a ticket. In fact, he said we all might be getting one. He went on to tell me that it is illegal to drive in these weather conditions and that I should have known better.

He was right. I should have known better; right then, however, the last thing I was worried about was getting a ticket. I even laughed a little when he said that, and I am sure that didn't help our situation any.

Jessica and Connie were crying again, and I was trying to make light of what had just happened. I am sure I was in a state of shock and didn't actually comprehend it myself, yet I just kept assuring those two that we would be all right.

Before night-fall we were towed into town, where we were put up in the armory overnight. Several people had come in off the interstate, and we were all given a cot to sleep on, some blankets to keep us warm and a good meal to tide us over until morning. It was very generous of the local people to take us in.

It was a sleepless night for me, filled with tossing and turning, and racing thoughts, and a jumble of mixed emotions. I was thankful that Jeremy was not with me, that the three of us had not been injured and that I had not been killed when I began to get out of the truck. If I had opened that door a second sooner and had been outside our truck, I could have been crushed when that semi-trailer hit us.

I was worried about what I would see when the sun came up and about what I was going to do next. I was close to crying but determined not to. I couldn't stop thinking about how bad South Dakota had been to me; first Matt hit the deer here years ago, and now this accident had happened. I couldn't stop wondering if this was a sign of things to come.

Chapter Seventeen

By morning the storm had died down, and we went to assess the damage. The tow truck driver, a local farm boy in his mid-20's with sandy brown hair had come to the Armory early to get us. He had a sympathetic look on his face as he came to find us in our corner of the building. I could tell he didn't really know what to say. I put on a good front, smiled at him, and asked for the damage report. He looked at me, even more sympathetically, and said, "It isn't good. Why don't you come look for yourself."

We all climbed into the cab of his tow truck; Jessica sat on my lap. The sun was shining brightly and the new coat of snow looked beautiful. The clear, crisp day provided little evidence of the brutal storm that had passed through the day before.

As we drove into the lot, the first thing I saw was my Datsun completely gnarled up in its trailer. It was up on a flatbed truck in the parking lot, and it was totally destroyed. You could barely tell it had been a car. Being without a car is a situation I don't deal with very well, and all I could do was hold my hands over my face and sigh. My Datsun was the only nice thing I had ever owned in my life, and now it was gone.

The tour wasn't over; he took us over to the U-Haul. It was beyond repair and we would not be able to leave town until another one was delivered later that day. The men at this station were very helpful, especially with the process of getting me another truck. Quite a crowd had gathered that morning to view the wreckage, and many people, including me, were surprised that we had survived the crash that had produced this destruction.

The day went by quickly because most of the things I had packed in the U-Haul had to be thrown away. It was all destroyed in the crash. I didn't have anything of great value, but it was still painful to clean out that truck and throw its contents into the dumpster. Every box that I had packed ended up being thrown away. I salvaged a few mementos, some pictures and my clothes. Other than that, everything had been destroyed: from dishes to furniture to knick-knacks, it was all gone.

Before we could leave, there were pictures to be taken, insurance people to talk to and family members to call. I hadn't made any calls the night before; I just wasn't up to it.

By 3:00 that afternoon, exactly 24 hours after the crash, we were back on I-90 heading west. The new U-Haul was smaller and much easier to drive. As I was going down the exit ramp to the freeway, I was tempted to go back to Minnesota and just give up. The only thing that kept me moving forward was Jeremy.

The rest of the trip was relatively uneventful. I don't think I relaxed, though, until we reached Eugene, Oregon. I was still in a bit of shock from the accident and just wanted to reach my destination. Jessica and Connie were afraid of every little weather change, and I needed to put on a strong front for them. Needless to say, I was pretty worn out by the time we arrived at Faith and Jim's.

Within a month we had found a place to rent in Springfield, and I was back working at a pizza place. After traveling so many miles down those freeways, I was back to where I had been when I first found out I was pregnant: working at a restaurant in Oregon.

Restaurant work didn't satisfy me any longer, and I found I had little tolerance left for it. While I was working I was crabby because I hated the job and hated facing the fact that this was all I knew how to do. While I was at home I was crabby because I knew I would have to leave for work soon.

I had to do something to change my line of work and went to see an employment service. They found me a job as a cashier who would also be helping out in the clothing department at a locally owned retail store. I was thrilled to be out of the restaurant business.

It took only a few months before Matt and I realized we were not going to make it. I tried as hard as I could to love him, as a wife should, but I just couldn't force it to happen. He tried to make believe I was someone that I wasn't. We both concluded at about the same time that it just was not going to work out between us. It was kind of a sad day, and yet it was also rather liberating. Our greatest challenges would be Jeremy and finances. In fact, we decided to live together for about another month, or so, until we could get our act together and figure out how we were going to proceed.

We went to the court-house, filled out a one-page divorce settlement, and within ten minutes it was done. We were no longer married. We were both rather ignorant about this, and we made no stipulations as to custody, child support or anything else. We didn't have any money to hire an attorney and just filed for a quick divorce. I still was not thinking about the future or the repercussions of my actions.

We agreed that Jeremy would stay with me; it was now Matt's turn to run away. He moved to a town about two hours south of where we were. His best friend was there, and he found a job. We didn't see him, or hear anything from him, for about six months. I can understand why he stayed away that long. Sometimes, it is just too painful to face situations.

～

Life was a daily struggle. We didn't receive any financial support from Matt because he didn't have it to give. And, as noted, we hadn't stipulated anything about Jeremy's care, or support or well-being anywhere in the divorce papers.

Daycare and rent were killing me. We had been living in a two-bedroom townhouse that was affordable with two salaries. My income alone, however, was just enough to pay for our rent and my daycare bill. I hated being really poor again, poor like when I was growing up. Things had always been financially tight for me and this reminded me of the situation I had been in as a young teenager. There was no extra money for anything and I was getting behind on some bills, mainly utilities.

I had no choice but to get a second job to make ends meet. The challenge was that this increased the daycare bill and it was like a catch 22. I had no family nearby to assist me, and I didn't really feel as though I could go to Faith and Jim for help. They had already done so much for me that I didn't want to go back and ask for more. However, they did baby-sit whenever they were able. That helped tremendously, because I was working odd hours and most weekends. I was too proud, though, to ask for any help beyond that.

I was determined to improve the life that I had brought Jeremy into, but I had no idea how I was going to make that happen. Up to this point his life had been chaotic and yet he was still a happy, loveable child. There were many days when I had no idea how I was going to make it. The road I had chosen was tough, but one look at him and his smile would encourage me. Often, when he could tell I was sad, he would come over and give me a hug or crawl up on my lap and kiss me. I don't know what I did to deserve such a great kid!

We talked every day about my love for him and my promise that things were going to get better for us. As far back as I can remember, I never wanted Jeremy thinking less of himself because of the situation that we were in, as I had during my childhood. I have always tried to help him understand the events going on around us and affecting our lives, and to assure him that, regardless of all of it, I would always love him and be here for him.

Our diet consisted mostly of fried egg sandwiches and Ramen Noodles, which was about all I could afford. I was always thankful for daycare, because they fed him well. He was still on a lot of baby food, and that helped, too. I would come home after a long day of work and stare at my empty cupboards wishing there was a way to get food in there.

I usually hated going to the mailbox because of the bills I'd find there. There were some doctor bills due to Jeremy's check-ups, and we didn't have medical insurance. There was car insurance to pay and just general living expenses. I didn't have any credit cards, which is probably a good thing, because they would have buried me. My phone bill was always high due to my checking on family members in Minnesota.

How things were going back there depended on the week that I called. They still relied heavily on my guidance, but they'd have to learn to do without it. I was too far away to really help, though I tried to support them the best I could. None of them had any idea how hard I was struggling. But then, it wouldn't have mattered if they did. What could they do to help?

I felt extremely guilty about the situation with Matt. It took me years to forgive myself for what happened. While in many ways I had been a victim of circumstances growing up, Matt became a victim of me. Yes, he was an adult and he made decisions for himself, but I still felt responsible for hurting him and for our breakup. I always felt responsible for the things that took place around me. Whether it was valid or not, I was ready to step in and take the heat. Perhaps this explains why I am consistently hard on myself; to this day I struggle with feeling that I don't deserve good things or success. I was ashamed of how I let Jeremy go, yet we were back together and I had to survive.

Bills that I couldn't pay were piling up. It was an endless cycle of deciding which bills to pay each month and which ones to let go. Thankfully, I didn't have a car payment. My car was an old 1980 Honda Civic; a faded, red two-door hatchback with lots of miles on it. It was not a pretty car, but it got me where I needed to go, it was reliable, and it got good gas mileage.

Jeremy and I would have to move, soon, though if I didn't figure something out. I couldn't afford to stay where we were, and I couldn't come up with a deposit and a first month's rent to move anywhere else. It was infuriating to feel that helpless. It seemed that everywhere I turned there was another dead end; I vowed to myself, and to Jeremy, that if we ever started climbing out of the hole we were in, I would never allow myself to return to it.

I didn't have the time or the confidence to have friends. However, there was someone I worked with who became an important part of our lives. His name was John and he had recently been released from alcohol/drug treatment and was trying to get his life back together. He had been in and out of several treatment centers, but he seemed determined to make it work this time. We started out simply as friends; just two people looking for companionship. Eventually, our relationship turned into more than just friendship.

We started out just chatting at work, and then started spending a little time together outside of work. He would stop over to visit and just sit and watch television with us, or, if Jeremy was at Faith and Jim's, we might go out for a drive around the Eugene/Springfield area. We were not heading any place specific, we just got in the car and drove. He was great with Jeremy and had a big, compassionate heart.

Chapter Eighteen

Before long, John and I were romantically involved even though we both were pretty leery of relationships. I was floundering through life and so was he, both trying to find our way. He needed a place to live and wasn't sure he could find anything he could afford. He had been living with his parents after his in-patient treatment, and it was time for him to move out. Mentally and emotionally, he needed to get out of there.

Meanwhile, I was still having trouble making ends meet and thought having a room-mate might be the only way we could stay in our townhouse. I had quit my second job because I just couldn't pay the daycare bills; debt was piling up and I knew that I wouldn't have the money to pay the next month's rent.

We decided that John would move in with us; we both felt that there was nothing to lose. It would help both of us financially and we were together all of the time anyway, so it seemed to make sense. In hindsight, it was too early in our relationship to do this, but, once again, I was in survival mode.

John's sponsor (from the treatment center) warned him that it was too soon for him to be in a relationship. Most programs suggest that a recovering addict be out of treatment for at least a year before entering into a serious relationship, and John had been out for only about six months. But, I needed a way to make ends meet, and this seemed to solve the problem. We split the bills 50/50 and he helped baby-sit Jeremy when he could.

We had the same challenges and difficulties that any couple faces, yet we both fell in love. He was working on his sobriety and I was working on improving life for Jeremy. With John in our lives, things seemed to be better. Money was not as tight as it had been, we had someone to spend time with and to bring joy into our lives. John spent hours playing with Jeremy and being my friend.

It was really exciting when we had made enough money to be able to move into an actual house; a cute little two-bedroom place over in Eugene that we rented. It had a garage, a fenced backyard, a deck off the dining area and a beautiful tree in the front yard. I was so happy that I cried tears of joy the day that we moved in. Things were going really well and it kind of scared me.

John had been promoted and was making decent money. We bought a couple of new cars, some nice things for our house and even a dog for Jeremy. John's family had welcomed us into their lives and we all reaped the benefits of that. Holidays came and went without any of my family around, but that was OK. In fact, it was probably better that way. The strings that had bound us had relaxed considerably in the years that I had been gone.

I wanted to get out of retail, but I didn't really want to go to college, so I attended a local business college. It was a nine-month program for business management, and I excelled in that environment. It was great to challenge my mind and work towards something, rather than simply trying to stay afloat. It also allowed me to meet some new people. Even though our lives had improved, I still was not very open to letting many people get close to me and I kept my guard up rather solidly. I never shared anything about my past or my family or my dreams. Even John didn't know much about my family life back home, and I chose to keep it that way.

Upon registering for school I was given a scholarship form from a local volunteer group called Soroptimist International. They were a group of women in business who gathered monthly to network and raise awareness of the needs of women in the workplace.

They offered a scholarship each year to someone in need, in each of several different categories. I fell into the young, single-mom category. The process was to fill out an application and get a letter of recommendation from someone in the business world.

That was easy to do. I went to a former employer, who graciously wrote a glowing recommendation about me. The year was 1990, and I won the scholarship! I was tremendously excited that I was the recipient of their grant. It allowed me to pay off my school loan, and it was the first time that I recall someone believing in my ability to succeed in life.

That spring I graduated with a 4.0 average and felt that I had a whole new life ahead of me. I was sure that that degree was all I would need to go out and find the career that was right for me. I still had a lot to learn.

In the job market, my degree didn't mean a whole lot. Sure, it helped me with my confidence, but it didn't mean much to the people who interviewed me. I was turned down numerous times and was really disappointed. Finally, however, I found a job with an advertising company in downtown Eugene.

It was a straight-commission sales position. My job was to get companies to advertise in a weekly bulletin. I had never been in sales before, not "real" sales. In retail, you just wait in the store for people to walk in. I had never worked on commission before, and it was an entirely new concept for me.

My role was to go out and talk to business people around town and acquire their business. I was scared to death, yet at the same time I felt an excitement that I had never felt before. This was my chance to prove myself and to be in the business world I had always longed to be a part of. I can still remember how I felt as I drove into the parking lot on my first morning, carrying my new briefcase, (a gift from John's family), all dressed up in business attire and ready to go to work. I felt I had a new lease on life.

That feeling quickly dissipated. As time went by, I learned that the company that had hired me was not very reputable. Three months into my job, with no paycheck yet, I went to work and found that the office was closed up and everything had been moved out. My boss had skipped town and I no longer had a job.

There had been only one client who was close to working with me, and I decided I should go see him and tell him the news. It was always nice to go see Rich anyway. He was a good guy, and I always enjoyed chatting with him.

Rather humbly I went in and told Rich what had happened and that I wouldn't be coming around anymore. He was the manager of Color Tile, a home improvement retail chain, and he asked me if I wanted a job. Without much thought, I said yes, and was back in retail. This time, though, I was a commissioned retail salesperson and would be working with people on improving their homes. It actually sounded like it would be rather fun.

I was quite successful at Color Tile. I was making more money than I ever had before, I liked my job and the people I worked with, and I was learning skills for working with people and the art of sales. We were one of the busiest stores in the country, and Rich took me under his wing and watched out for me in the men's world of home improvement sales.

In addition, Jeremy was thriving in our new, stable environ-ment. He was doing well in daycare and was a joy to come home to. He loved his puppy, had a group of neighborhood kids that he liked to play with and loved to be read to. We spent hours upon hours reading books together and found that was one of our favorite activities together.

John spent four evenings a week at AA meetings and going out for coffee afterwards. I didn't always understand why he had to attend so many meetings and we sometimes argued about it. I knew nothing about addiction. Even though I had been surrounded by it as a youth, that word had never come up. Mom had been addicted to her Tylenol, and I'm sure I was close to being an alcoholic at one time. Many of the people I surrounded myself with back home were either hard drinkers, pot-heads or both. But, I had never known anyone who had been hooked on cocaine, as John had been.

I finally grasped how important it was for him to attend the meet-ings, but I still didn't understand why he had to go sit in a coffee shop for a couple of hours after each meeting, with the same group of peo-ple. I took it personally, as if he didn't want to be around home—and that was a mistake. In reality, John was just trying to take care of himself.

We did our best to keep the lines of communication open between us. But, without my even consciously realizing it, John began coming home later and later after his meetings. I occasionally asked him about it, whereupon he pointed the finger at me. He began to tell me how I was the one who needed help and, stupidly, I let his messages sink in. I didn't know that I was being manipulated. I was taking the blame for what was going on then. Thinking that I was being too demanding, I backed off and decided to just let his late nights go.

One night in November 1990, John didn't come home until 4:00 A.M. I had been awake since midnight and was sitting on the couch waiting for him. He had never come home this late; 2:00 was common, but never 4:00, and I was really worried about him. I didn't know where he was, who he was with or what was going on. All I knew is that he wasn't home yet and as each hour went by my concern and frustration were mounting.

The minute he opened the door and walked in I knew that he was high; John had relapsed and had snorted some cocaine. He was surprised to see me up and became defensive when I asked him where he had been. He didn't feel that he had to share any-thing with me, and within moments he was crawling into bed as if nothing had happened.

I followed John into our bedroom and, I tried to talk to him, I realized that he was not responding. He wasn't just ignoring me—there was no response whatsoever; he had slipped into unconsciousness. John is a diabetic and needs to take insulin shots several times a day. While he was out having "fun," he'd forgotten to take his insulin shots and was crashing, hard.

Beyond being exasperated with him for relapsing, I was now concerned for his life. There had been occasions when John, straight and sober, had experienced reactions to insulin and had been put in the hospital. However, I had never seen him completely pass out before. I tried to wake him, but couldn't. I knew that if something wasn't done very quickly, he could slip into a coma. Frantically, I called two of his brothers to come and help me.

Both of them lived only minutes away from our house; both were disgusted when they arrived. They had seen this kind of thing with John too many times before and just couldn't believe that he had done it again. They carried him to the car and took him to the hospital. I stayed home; Jeremy was still sleeping, and there wasn't anything I could do for John at that point.

As they drove away, I started to cry. I didn't understand why John would do this or how he could relapse after all the time he'd spent in AA meetings. I was hurt and disappointed, and I felt that maybe I had done something to cause him to start using again or that I should have been able to prevent it. Whatever the cause, it was a complete shock to me that John had done this. I thought things had been going well between us. I thought our lives had been coming together and our future had been looking bright.

By 5:30 A.M. we knew that John was going to be OK. The hospital said that he would be able to come back home that afternoon, and that was a relief. However, his hospital visit was only a small part of what had happened. The bigger issue was, "Now what?"

As I was getting myself ready for work and Jeremy for daycare, I was determined to remain strong. There was no way I would let Jeremy know what was going on, so I just told him that John had gone into the office early that morning. My emotions had gone from anger to panic to grief and somewhere, inside of me, I had to find the strength to get through this day. As we left the house that morning and crawled into our car, I had no idea what our life would be like when we returned home that afternoon.

It was a gloomy day at work. I did my best to put up a good front, but Rich and a co-worker, Steve, knew something was very wrong. They had been aware of some of my frustrations at home for some time and had been trying to convince me that I deserved better than John. We had spent hours talking about my situation, yet, as hard as they now tried to assure me it wasn't so, I still believed that whatever was going wrong was somehow my fault.

Chapter Nineteen

After John came home, he and I did our best to put the incident behind us. John insisted that his relapse was a one-time thing and that he was ready to go back to working on overcoming his addiction. I wanted to believe him, and I did my best to put our life back together the way it had been. We flew back to Minnesota to spend Christmas with my family, and everything appeared to be going well. None of them knew anything about the relapse, and I wanted to keep it that way.

John was back in the routine of attending meetings and coming home by 10:00 P.M. We continued to avoid discussing the relapse and went on with life. By April of 1991, he was back to using cocaine on a regular basis.

I should have seen the warning signs and didn't. Or maybe I did and tried to ignore them. He was out most nights, slept most days, and I caught him in several lies. He was in danger of losing his job and it didn't even phase him. I would see him around town with people I didn't recognize, and a couple of times he even had the nerve to drive down the road near our home with other women. On one occasion, I was entering our subdivision as he was leaving it, and we met at the intersection. There was a young girl in the car with him, and I played it cool, said hello and drove on home. The next day, when he came home, he acted as if I had no right to question him about the girl or what they were doing together. I didn't know what to do. Any time I confronted him, he would lie to me. I desperately wanted to believe that everything was OK with him, but, clearly, it wasn't. Our money started to disappear, and we began fighting on a regular basis.

I was not a happy person. I had thought that things were getting better for me. I had thought that life couldn't continue to be so cruel to me. I had thought that John and I would live a long happy life together. We had never really discussed marriage, but we had planned to purchase a home together and were making plans for our future. That changed in an instant. I pleaded with John to get help;

he told me he would. He didn't. I asked him why he was doing this to us and he would storm out. He would show up the next day and apologize, and I would forgive him. I was trying to will him to get better. Unfortunately, it doesn't work that way.

Meanwhile, there were increasing problems at home, in Minnesota. Mom had tried to commit suicide again, and Tim and Jessica were calling regularly to ask for help. By the middle of May I was packing up my car and along with Jeremy getting ready for the long drive back to Minnesota. I had decided to go home to try to help the family, and to also give myself a couple of weeks to clear my mind and to give John some space. I didn't know how long I would be gone, but my boss, Rich, told me to take as much time as I needed. It wouldn't be a paid vacation, but my job would be waiting for me when I returned.

John happened to stop at home when we were packing. Although, I am sure I had mentioned to him that we were going to Minnesota for a visit, he wasn't in a very good mood when he discovered what was going on. It didn't matter how he reacted. The pressure had been hitting me from all angles, and I had determined that the best thing to do was to take some time, go help my family and, I hoped, figure out my life.

Jeremy was just great on the three-day drive. This time I could afford a motel room to sleep in, which made the trip much more endurable. Which is not to say it was pure pleasure. During that entire trip I felt extremely stressed; I was becoming little more than a walking bundle of raw nerves. Once again, I was just trying to survive.

We ended up staying in Minnesota for 2½ weeks before driving back to Oregon. Jessica and Tim had been thrilled to have that much time with us and it did me good to get away from John's influence. They still didn't know what was really going on with me, and I didn't tell them. They were having enough challenges of their own, and I didn't want to worry anyone.

Before heading back on Interstate 80 once again, I had determined that I was going to go back and make the best of things. I was confident that John's relapse and aberrant behavior were just temporary, and that things would be better by the time I got back.

I also had decided to invite Tim to come out and live with us for a while. Things weren't going so well for him, and he was looking for a change, so he took me up on it. Even though our home was small, it did have three bedrooms and Tim was more than welcome to join us. I was actually thrilled about this. It would be good for him to get away from his environment for a while and good for me and Jeremy to spend some time with him. The plan was for Tim to come out in about a week.

The drive back to Oregon was uneventful, but when we arrived, within moments of entering our home I knew that John had not improved. He was passed out in our bed, the house was a mess, and he looked like hell. I'm not sure what I expected, but at that point in my life I didn't understand the power of addiction. I did not know what addiction can do to a person.

I felt crushed when I saw John and our home's disarray. I also felt that my only option was to kick him out. I hated the way John looked at me and spoke to me. Even though I was hurting inside there was no way I was going to let him see it. I had no idea what was going to happen next, I just knew he had to leave.

I relied on John's family for support, but in fact, none of us really knew what to do with him. They had been through this so many times with him in the past that they had given up hope of his ever changing. Now he had lost his job (for not showing up), and even though I had kicked him out, he would stop by once a week to check in, eat and get money. The frustrating thing is, I let him do it.

In the meantime, I had heard about a program called Alanon, for family members of addicts. I went to a meeting but decided that it wasn't for me. They were talking about co-dependency issues and enabling our loved ones and, in my ignorance, I thought that I didn't need the information that they were sharing. How wrong I was.

Tim did make it out to live with us, but within about a month he was moving back to Minnesota. I wanted him to stay and make it work, probably more for my sake than his, but he just wasn't happy. He missed his friends and, looking back honestly, I think he was disappointed to how I was allowing John to use me. He wasn't the only one.

On about the fourth of July Tim packed up his truck to head back to Minnesota. My life was in shambles, but I believed that John would overcome his drug problem and our lives would return to normal some day soon. In fact, he had agreed to go through treatment again and had checked himself in to a detox center a couple of days before Tim left. He would be in the treatment center for a few weeks and had asked for my support through that time. He seemed serious about straightening out his life, and I was thrilled that he was taking this step.

For some reason, that I can't recall—maybe simply to run away— Jeremy and I joined Tim on his drive back to Minnesota. The three of us piled in his truck for another long drive half-way across the country. It allowed me to get away for a few days and to see how things were going with mom at home. It was going to be a little spendy for us to fly back to Oregon; I felt it was worth it. I convinced myself that by the time Jeremy and I returned home in a week or so things would be looking brighter for us.

～

By September I was at my wits end. Within a few days of finishing treatment, John had gone back to using. He came home whenever he felt like it, I would tell him to not return, but he would anyway. I changed the locks to our home. Then, foolishly, during one of his visits, I let him talk me into giving him a key. I grew to dread seeing him, yet I still cared for him and felt that somehow I could make this all better. I still was not quite ready to completely close the door on our relationship. I would start to close it part-way, only to open it wide for a false promise or a blatant lie.

I was hurting emotionally and financially; 1991 had been a tough year and it didn't seem to be improving. John's addiction was as strong as ever and it was wiping me out financially. Sure, I was still making a decent income and his parents were helping out where they could but, it was not enough.

John had begun to make some reckless decisions. He had taken things from our home to sell for drug money, had cleared out our savings and checking accounts, had maxed out our credit card for a cash advance and had even tried to sell our car. I had not taken the steps to separate any of our accounts, and my name was still on the title to the car. The dealership needed my signature before they could proceed with the transaction, and I refused to provide it.

John's brother had driven me to the dealership; when I arrived back home with the Toyota, John was sitting there waiting for me. He was angry and we got into a heated argument. Asking him to leave hadn't seemed to do any good in the past, because he always came back—but, once again, our argument concluded with him driving away after I insisted that he leave.

I walked into our home, through the living room and kitchen and went out the sliding glass doors to go and sit on the deck. The sun was shining, and the temperature was a comfortable 70 degrees; it was a beautiful fall day, yet I was a wreck. Thankfully, Jeremy was at daycare and wasn't around to see any of this; it was that afternoon that I finally hit rock bottom. I sat and cried for what seems like hours.

I am often asked what it's like to hit "rock bottom." It's difficult to explain. I believe that hitting rock bottom happens when a person finally sees reality for what it is versus what he or she wants it to be. When I came home from that car dealership, I was aghast at the way

John was behaving. I had never seen anything like it before; he seemed to be filled with a vengeance that had not been there previously. The effect that cocaine, or for that matter any abused drug, can have on an individual is devastating. Even more devastating is the effect this drug use has on the innocent people in the abuser's life.

Our money was gone and John was making my life miserable, but the thing that hit me the hardest was the realization that I was raising my son in a terribly unhealthy environment. I had vowed to improve our lives; sitting on that deck in the afternoon sunshine, I realized that I had not been following through on that promise. For the past nine months I had buried my head in the sand and hoped things would improve. However, I had never taken responsibility, complete responsibility, for making the improvement happen. I was crushed when I realized that my life had become exactly what I hadn't wanted it to. How did I get in such a mess?

While I felt shattered, I also felt exhilarated. There is a wise old saying that, "The first step to improvement is awareness," and I believe that is what started to happen that afternoon. For some reason, at that moment I was finally ready to become aware of my situation, to take responsibility for it. The reality I saw wasn't pleasant.

Part Three

The Road Home

Chapter Twenty

The first decision I had to make was where we were going to live. Originally, I had come to the conclusion that we would stick it out in Eugene, Oregon and somehow survive. I didn't have family around, but Jeremy's grandparents were there, and, even though his father didn't live with us, he was still in the same state. As weeks passed, however, it became increasingly clear to me that in order to get away from John, and his malice towards life, we would have to move away. Otherwise, he would continue to manipulate me.

The decision to move back to my home, to Minnesota, was one of the most difficult I have ever had to make. My objective was to create a "good" life to raise my son in and so far, I hadn't accomplished that. I didn't want to take Jeremy away from his relatives, but I didn't have any alternative. Somewhere, deep in my soul, I felt that I needed to go back to where I began and start anew. Today I would consider it a message from God, but at that time I wasn't aware of that possibility. It may have given me more confidence if I had been.

I talked with Jeremy's grandparents and explained the situation. They hadn't been aware of John's drug problem and seemed to understand my decision. Telling Matt didn't go as smoothly; it was the hardest part of leaving. We all make choices, and he had chosen not to be involved with Jeremy since I had moved out there in 1989. We had never received any financial support from him. Even so, I didn't want to take Jeremy away from his father, but I couldn't see any other options.

With that done, we were making plans to move in mid-October. I was starting over again, but this time I was going to be wiser about it. I ensured a job transfer to a Color Tile in the Minneapolis area and was shipping our belongings, bit by bit, back to my grandparent's home. That way, I wouldn't have to be pulling a trailer when we hit the freeway.

I went through the actions of paying off and canceling the utilities, phone and every other service we had so that when I left I was not leaving anything undone. It felt great to be taking some action. I was scared to death and yet, just by simply doing something, I felt better about myself and my life.

Before long, John found out we were moving away. He had stopped by occasionally and could see that I was packing some things up and moving. It didn't take a rocket scientist to figure out where I was moving to, and he was quite cynical about my taking that step.

One day, while I was at work, John decided that he didn't want me to take much back to Minnesota. He went into my home and took things that he felt were his: the microwave, stereo, television, wall hangings—you name it, he took it. It did help with my shipping bill, but that was no comfort at all.

I was furious when Jeremy and I walked in to find most of our things gone. These were items that I was hanging on to until right before we left. They were items that we needed on a daily basis, and now they were gone. I could not believe that he had stooped to that level and yet, in hindsight, it was predictable.

Sometimes a person can feel that things are so bad that there is no way they can get worse. Well, at this point, it had gotten worse. I felt like giving up on life and quitting; throwing in the towel and simply accepting that this was as good as it was going to get for me and Jeremy. I am sure many of us have experienced days like that; I believe the thing that keeps us going is hope.

Some of us learn more slowly than others, and it seems as though I always have to learn things the hard way. My soul was really tired of being beaten up, but I reminded myself that I had chosen to take responsibility for my life since that day in September.

By no means am I taking responsibility for John's relapse. However, I am taking responsibility for my choice to get involved with him even when I had been warned about the repercussions; for the fact that I put my son into that environment when I should have figured things out on my own. If my life was going to become better, and therefore Jeremy's life as well, it had to start with me.

It was a sad day. I had lost everything—again—but I still had Jeremy and I still had hope for a brighter future. Each day of our lives we can choose to make the most of what we have, or to hang out the white flag of surrender. I had been a fighter my entire life, and at that point, I wasn't about to stop. Besides, I was sure there was only one way to go from where I was: up.

For too many years I had been looking for someone else to make me happy and to straighten out my life instead of doing it myself, and look where it had gotten me. Recently, I found a quote that sums up what I'd learned: "God will only give us more when we have taken care of what we've got." I had to take care of what "I'd got".

Part of that was setting some boundaries with my family before I moved back home. I talked to each of my siblings, at length, to make sure they knew I was not coming back to take care of them. They knew about John's troubled past, but this was the first they had heard of his relapse.

Mom was happy that we were coming back, we also had a long discussion about my reason for moving back. It had nothing to do with taking care of her and her life. Granted, I will always be the one who talks with her social worker and deals with the various programs that we have her on, but my motive for coming back was purely personal: to start at the beginning and fix things.

They all still lived in the Deerborne area, and I made a conscious decision to live in the Twin Cities metropolitan area, about an hour away from them. Nathan had been living in the metro area for some years and he found us a place to live. It was an apartment that was the lower level of a home. There was a single father of three living upstairs, and he was looking for someone to help pay the mortgage. There was only one kitchen, so we shared that and the entryway into the home. Other than that, the lower level of the home was ours.

That day in mid-October when we were finally leaving was an exciting one. There's a feeling you get when you know you are doing the right thing, when you can just feel with all your being that you are going in the right direction. It's an incredibly exciting feeling. I was moving, again on a wing and a prayer, but this time, I was going back to face my challenges instead of running farther away from them.

For the third time that year we were heading down Highway 20, which would lead us to Interstate 84 which would take us to the now familiar Interstate 80. This move, though, was a much smoother trip than my other moves.

We did not incur any accidents, deer or bad weather. I felt wonderful, almost ecstatic, as we cruised down the road. At the same time, I was scared to death and listened to all sorts of doubts running through my mind: "What if this isn't the right thing to do?" "What if I'm making another mistake?" "What if things don't work out?" "What if Jeremy hates me, someday, for taking him away from his father?"

I think I had every self-limiting belief I could have had those few days on the road; any and every possible negative thought that I could have had intruded on my consciousness. I didn't understand it then, but I do now, that that's a normal reaction to change. Any time we step out and create a new life for ourselves there will, initially, be lots of negative forces that can stop us in our tracks if we let them. The key is to not let them interfere and to forge ahead with your intended plans. In fact, at that point, I had nothing to lose by doing what I was doing.

~

Once again, my greatest daily struggle was making ends meet. Jeremy was adapting to his new daycare and the life we were living. It is amazing how kids often make transitions much more comfortably than adults.

My job was going well, although this store did not have nearly the volume that the one in Eugene did, and so, my paychecks were smaller and my bills were larger. John ran up a huge debt on the credit card, and the payments were murder. Added to that were my car payment, rent and daycare. We were back to the lifestyle we had lived, pre-John.

There were many times when I had no idea what we were going to eat that night for supper. On numerous occasions, after making sure Jeremy was fed, I got by on a piece of toast or a fried egg sandwich. I had burned out on the ramen noodles years ago and couldn't even force myself to eat them. Living like this is a struggle. The never-ending concern about money begins to wear on you and, before you know it, you have an expectation of always being poor.

There were other challenges also. My family did not adapt very well to the new me. They did not like the fact that I was not accessible to them 24 hours a day, seven days a week. They did not like the fact that I was not here to care for them and fix their lives. It took all of us quite some time to adapt to the boundaries that I had set. In my heart, I wanted to do more for them, but I couldn't allow myself to.

There were many times it was excruciating to take a step back and not get involved with Jessica's or Tim's life. I had to remind myself constantly that I was here to take care of myself and my son and that was it. I also had to make myself realize that that was OK; it wasn't that I didn't care about them, I just couldn't take on their lives. I had enough to deal with on my own.

I do need to note, though, that I will be forever grateful to Jessica, Tim and mom for helping me out with daycare when they could. I was still working lots of weekends and they did their part to help out where they could.

The greatest challenge I faced was to not fall back into my old routines and patterns. I started to read some books on codependency, and it is amazing how I fit into that mode at one point in my life. I started to realize that I had choices to make each and every day of my life. I also started to realize that I needed to start looking at those choices for long-term solutions rather than short-term fixes. I was determined to avoid having a man in my life for quite some time. I wanted, and needed, to do this on my own.

Chapter Twenty-One

In January 1992 I went to an employee party, even though I more or less intentionally had no social life. The manager (Tammy) of the West St. Paul store had come over to manage the Bloomington store where I worked. She had a party at her home to say good-bye to the "old" employees and hello to the "new". We had been working together for about a month or so before she had this party, and she is the kind of person who won't take "no" for an answer to an invitation.

Tammy had an ulterior motive that I was not aware of. She had been trying for some time to set me up on a date with a fellow who worked at her previous store. I kept telling her I wasn't interested, but she didn't listen. She knew that this man, Pat, would be at her party and that is why she kept insisting that I attend.

Since Tammy planned the party, she was able to finagle situations in which Pat and I couldn't avoid interacting. For one thing, she had assigned seating and—surprise—Pat and I were seated next to one another. Also, in any game that was played, Pat seemed to end up as my partner. While it was a little uncomfortable, I must say I rather enjoyed the evening.

Pat wasn't a total stranger to me. I had talked with him on the phone a few times, about store supplies. Once, I had to go to his store for something and had actually met him, and he seemed like a pleasant person. But I just was not looking for anyone at that point. God must have had a different plan for me.

Within a few days of that party, Pat called and asked me out on a date. He had to go to Duluth for a few days on business, but he wanted to see me when he got back home. He knew I had a son, but that didn't deter him; he just wanted to go out for a bite to eat.

I was hesitant on the phone, but I finally agreed, though I told him that I was not looking for a relationship at that point. He said he felt the same way and we agreed to touch base when he returned to town.

It was about a week before we went out, and I was scared to death. I didn't want to get hurt again, or to repeat the patterns that had gotten me in trouble in the past. I needed to "take care of what I got" before I moved into anything else. And yet Pat seemed like such a terrific person. How could I say no to someone like him?

He was 30 years old, had never been married, didn't have any children and had been born and raised in Hastings, the same town my sister Jessica had been born in. He had only moved away for a short time while he was going to College. He had lived what I call a "leave it to beaver" type of life. Pat's upbringing and life had been as far as you can get from what I had experienced.

Before our first date I had decided to handle this differently from the very beginning. Jeremy would not be involved in this right away. There was no way I was going to risk hurting my son again. He had been through enough in his short life, and I was not going to bring another person into his life who could possibly hurt him. He had done amazingly well with this recent upheaval, and I just wanted to protect him better than I had previously.

Our first date was on Saturday, February 8, 1992. We met in Hastings and went out for dinner and then on to a party. Dinner was great and I immediately felt comfortable around Pat and he appeared to feel that way around me.

Pat shared his background with me and I shared a little bit with him. I was not going to hide my past from him, but I didn't want to dump it on him all at once. He knew that I had been married before, had grown up in Southern Minnesota, had lived out west for a while and now was back. I told him again, that I was not looking for a relationship.

Our first date was fun. We had a good time that night and he called the next day. We agreed to meet again for dinner later that week.

Even though I insisted to myself that I did not want a relationship, I found myself anxiously waiting for that second date.

We went to dinner and a movie. I shared a bit more with Pat about my history. Again, I wanted each of us to go into this with our eyes wide open. I didn't expect him to have any interest in me after he learned where I came from, but he still called me the next day.

It appeared that the little bit he knew didn't stop him from wanting to date me. Now I was really getting scared. I didn't want to get hurt again, yet Pat didn't have any "baggage" that he was carrying around, had a great personality, looked great and liked me for who I was. How could I close the door on this?

Pat had a planned trip to Jamaica with about 20 of his friends that March. He was gone for a little over a week, and I thought that would be the time he would decide he didn't want to see me anymore. I missed him while he was gone, but I was pretty guarded with my soul. I didn't want to raise any false hopes. It didn't seem possible that someone this good would be interested in me, yet when he arrived back in the Cities, he called and said he wanted to come over to see me.

He had never met Jeremy, and I was pretty apprehensive about that happening. I decided he could stop over after Jeremy was in bed. I had only known Pat for a couple of months and just did not want Jeremy involved. However, Pat showed up earlier than expected with a gift for Jeremy, a T-shirt from Jamaica, that he wanted to give him. I will never forget that evening.

The door bell rang and I ran up the stairs to answer the door. There was Pat with a smile on his face and gifts in his hands. It turned out he also brought back something for me. I greeted him with a rather shy "hello".

At the top of the stairs, we looked down and there was four-year-old Jeremy standing at the bottom of the steps in his winter sleeper pajamas, the one-piece kind with attached white feet. He turned to see who was coming down the steps and immediately got a really big smile on his face. He was curious who this man was, yet he greeted him with the warmth that only a four-year-old can generate.

When we reached the bottom, I introduced Pat to my son and let Jeremy open his gift. It fit him perfectly and I found that, though, I was touched, deep in my soul, I didn't want to be. It seems that sometimes the things that are best for me are the most frightening to me. It seemed like I was falling in love again, but this time it was very different. It was not one-sided, or based on financial need or desperation. It was a feeling of longing when we weren't together and a feeling of joy when we were.

Over the next few months Pat and I began to spend more and more time together. It got to the point where we were together most nights, and he suggested that we move in together. We were on opposite sides of the Cities and spent a lot of time on the road going back and forth between our homes.

My answer was a firm "no." My reason for coming back and starting over was to stop repeating the patterns that I had been through before. And there was no way ever again I would bring a man into Jeremy's life only to have him leave.

It is amazing how much you can improve your life by simply deciding to make it better. As I started to look at things differently, it seemed as if the whole world around me had changed. The world hadn't changed, I was just looking at things in a different light. Opportunities, possibilities and people are always there. It is simply up to us to see them and utilize them to the greatest benefit for all parties.

Chapter Twenty-Two

On Friday, October 16, 1992 Patrick and I were married. It had been a whirlwind romance, but we were both mature enough to know that the time was right. I believe in destiny and that he was someone that God brought into my life; a blessing, if you will.

Before we married I made sure he knew everything about me; my family and all the events that had taken place. Sometimes during our discussions he couldn't take hearing any more from me. Sometimes, we would end a phone conversation and I didn't know if I would hear back from him. Sometimes he would leave my home and I didn't know if I would ever see him again. My background was a lot for someone to accept, especially someone with the ideal background that Pat had had. He always came back, though. After he had some time to think things over, he always called me back.

Pat's friends and family could not believe he was getting married. Most of them had never met me, and he had always been a guy who was single and loved it. My grandpa was concerned I hadn't known him long enough to marry him. I can certainly understand all of those thoughts and emotions. And yet, how could I walk away from this wonderful person who had come into my life?

As a little girl I thought all it took to make things work was love. In my adult years I've learned it takes more than love. It takes commitment, similar values, wanting the same things out of life, and, in addition, a deep love for each other. Pat and I both admit that today, seven years later, we are even more in love than when we were married. Don't get me wrong; I was crazy about Pat. I was head-over-heals in love, and yet I would say at this point our love is more mature than it was that day in 1992.

Our wedding was small; we were on a tight budget and married in Hastings, at the church in which Jessica was baptized many years ago. I never would have guessed that I would be back living in Hastings. Out of all of the places I had been, here I end up falling in love with a man from Hastings.

I wore the dress that my mom wore at her first wedding and Grandpa Baker gave me away. I was so nervous I could hardly speak the wedding vows and yet, this felt like a marriage ought to feel. I didn't feel "trapped" as I had the first time around. I felt thankful, excited and joyful. In fact, in my heart Pat is the only husband I have ever had. I sometimes even forget that I was married before.

I had quit my job at Color Tile and went to work for a cable company in Rosemount. It provided regular hours and a stable paycheck, and it allowed me and Jeremy to get settled into Hastings.

We rented a town-home, got Jeremy registered to start preschool, found him a great daycare with a person who was referred to us, and our new life began. It seemed too good to be true. It happened so quickly, and yet it just felt right. Pat had accepted my son as his own and me with my distressed past.

It certainly was not without its challenges, though. Pat became a dad and a husband all at once. I was not financially stable; I brought a load of debt into our marriage along with the "baggage" I was carrying around from my past.

~

Before long I was getting restless at my job with the cable company. I have always had an itch, deep within my soul, to do something worthwhile with my life, to help other people and to utilize the unlimited energy that I seem to have. At that point, however, I didn't have an outlet for this deep inner desire to be something more than I was. Heck, I didn't even know how to define that urge or what it meant. I

just thought I was destined to be eternally hyperactive and unsatis-
fied with life. I could not define my feelings, emotions, desires or
dreams. I just knew that there had to be more.

In January 1993 I decided to go into real estate. I had been searching for something that would offer me unlimited potential and
independence. I never have done well working for other people, and I
used to think it was a flaw. I now think of it as a gift—as long as it is
used correctly.

I didn't receive my first paycheck until the following May, and by
that time Pat and I had decided that we needed to make some adjustments if we were going to survive financially. We had to downgrade
our monthly rental payment. This was tough. I hated giving up our
town-home and yet, a person has to do what he or she has to do to get
ahead.

It was another move, but this time it was just across town to an
apartment building. As anyone who has owned a small business
knows, it takes a long time and a lot of effort for benefits to start
accruing. In fact, the Small Business Administration consistently
reports that it takes an average of three to five years before a person
starting a business will be able to see any rewards. I did not know
that when I began my real estate career.

In addition to my career, I found myself wanting to make everything perfect for Jeremy and Pat. There was no way that I was going
to let anything else happen that would endanger our new-found happiness. I started to think about raising Jeremy in a family
environment that would support him and offer him opportunities as
he grew into adulthood. Pat and I discussed the importance of getting
Jeremy involved in church or Sunday school in order to gain some
idea of who God and Jesus are.

On the first Sunday of January in 1994 I decided to take Jeremy
to church, the same church in which Pat and I had been married 14
months earlier. I was pretty nervous about walking through those
doors; was afraid that entering the church would force me to face
myself, and I wasn't sure if I was up to that or not.

When mom was married to Brad we attended church, but I
went because I was told to. I had never felt a strong compulsion to
learn more about this person called Jesus, and now I was entering
His world.

Due to the holiday season there was no Sunday School that day,
which provided an easy excuse for us to cop out and go back home.
However, the next Sunday we went back, and we've been attending
ever since. That first visit of mine was filled with trepidation. I sat

as far back as I could during the service, so I wouldn't attract any attention to myself. Even though I was a realtor I was still relatively stand-offish towards people. Not a good trait to have in that career.

When the service was over I went to get Jeremy, and there was a gentleman there by the name of Gordon Gathright. He was, and still is, the youth pastor of our church. He came up to me, said hello, and introduced himself. He also told me that I was welcome to come back, and that he hoped he would see me again.

Gordon was the impetus for my discovery of this thing called faith. I certainly have no intention for this book to be an evangelical treatise. However, a large part of my becoming who I am today has been my walk of faith.

As I began attending church on a regular basis, I experienced unfamiliar feelings and struggles. My life was going well, comparatively speaking, yet I still did not have any inner peace, confidence, joy or real happiness. We all know, and have heard countless times, that you can never really love anyone until you love yourself. Well, I did not love myself, and until I learned to, things would remain the same.

When we moved into Hastings, my past pretty much disappeared. I closed those doors, locked them tight, and threw the key away. I never told anyone anything about my past. I felt that I would be judged for it and was not confident enough in myself to realize that that doesn't matter. True friends will accept you for who you are. I was not mature enough yet to know that.

I had some pretty big walls set up around my heart, my soul and my entire being. I was having some success in real estate, was making a comfortable living, was able to pay bills and reduce our debt. However, that infamous "chip" was still lodged on my shoulder, though I was unaware of it. I had never recognized that my attitude towards other people would affect the way people react towards me. I had never recognized the fact that I pushed people away instead of inviting them into my world. I had never recognized the fact that when there was conflict or disagreement, much of it had to do with me. I had never known that each and every one of us can gain control of our emotions and thoughts and destructive patterns.

As I was creating my new life, I found that I went through a phase where I was trying to do it all. I was working about 60+ hours a week to get my business going, while also trying to be a great wife and mom. I suppose I was trying to make up to Jeremy for all of the trials I had put him through.

In addition, I started to volunteer extensively throughout my church, my community, the school district and professional organizations. Without even realizing it, I was trying to prove my worth and make up for all the painful events that I had caused in my life by the choices I had made.

I was working pretty hard at getting people to approve of me and accept me. Whenever someone asked me to do something, I couldn't say no. If I did, major guilt would set in, and I felt awful. I thought that if I did more and more things to help other people, somehow it would make up for all the bad mistakes I had made in my life. Again, the fear of not being accepted was greater than the realization that I was wearing myself out.

Chapter Twenty-Three

One Sunday morning early in February 1994, at about 8:00 A.M., the phone rang. It was cold and blustery outside, and we had decided to stay home that morning, not go to church, and just enjoy the time we had with each other. I rarely had a Sunday free due to open houses, and this was truly going to be a day off for me.

When the phone began to ring, I couldn't figure out who would call this early on a Sunday morning. We only had one phone in the apartment, and I jumped out of bed and hurried down the hall to catch it before they hung up. I figured it must have been an important call and didn't want to miss it.

I picked up the phone, said "Hello" and on the other end a voice asked "Is Peggy there?"

I answered, " This is Peggy," and the voice on the other end said, "This is your father. I wanted to let you know that your grandfather died and the funeral is Tuesday with the visitation tomorrow evening. My mom told me to let you kids know. You are welcome to come if you wish. It is in Lynden at the funeral home. Please let your brothers and sister know."

I was stunned and had no idea how to respond to what I'd just heard. I was experiencing so many emotions, on all different levels, that I don't even recall what I said to him beyond the fact that I didn't commit to attending.

I said good-bye, hung up, and stood there literally shaking. I had not talked to my father since the day he had left 22 years earlier. I don't even know how he found me. My last name was different, we had just moved, and yet, somehow, he knew how to reach me. What makes this even more miraculous is that Nathan, Tim and Jessie had had some contact with him in previous years, yet dad chose to call me.

As Nathan got older he had seen dad a couple of times when he came up for family reunions, but a relationship never developed between them. While I was living in Oregon, Jessica and Tim decided they wanted to meet and know their father. They found out where he lived and one weekend they took a couple of friends and drove down to see him. There had been some further contact with him and yet, nothing developed between them, either.

I am not sure why nothing developed except for the fact that I don't think any of them knew how to proceed with each other. I was always the one who told all of them to leave me out of it. I didn't want them talking about me, showing pictures of Jeremy or anything. I was the one who was determined to stay away.

It had been a few moments since I got off the phone and Pat yelled from the bedroom asking who had been on the phone. As I started my slow descent down the hallway, I told him still a bit dazed, that it had been my dad.

Pat was, obviously, pretty surprised and met me in the hallway to see how I was reacting. He was curious as to what the call was about, and after I told him, neither of us really knew what to do.

Pat headed back to the bedroom and I went and sat in our living room chair, a bundle of nerves. What was I supposed to do? Was this something that was brought my way for a reason? Was God telling me that I needed to take care of what "I got"?

I sat there for about an hour hashing this over in my mind. I felt an inner compulsion to attend the visitation the next evening and couldn't shake the feeling that I needed to go. I called my brothers and sister, told them about the call and that we (Pat, Jer and I) were going to attend. I felt it was something that should be done out of respect for our grandfather. They agreed to join us, and we set a time and meeting place right outside of Fairview for the next afternoon.

Needless to say, I couldn't concentrate on much of anything for the next 32 hours. It is probably a good thing I had no work responsibilities that Sunday. We left Hastings the next day, Monday, at about 4:00 to meet my siblings at 5:00. The visitation was scheduled from 4:00 P.M. to 7:00 P.M. I didn't want us to be the first group there, but I didn't want to wait until the very end either. We thought if we were there by 5:30 that would be sufficient.

It was one of those really frigid Minnesota winter days. It would have been easy to use the weather as an excuse not to go. The wind was howling and the wind chill was well below zero. The roads were slippery due to a light snow that had fallen Sunday night. Nevertheless, I just couldn't back out. The thought was tempting, but I felt that this was something that I had to do. Nathan came to our place and rode down with us.

That drive to Lynden was one of the longest I had ever experienced. I don't think I had eaten anything since I received that phone call the morning before. We arrived at our meeting place, the parking lot of a Conoco truck stop about eight miles from Lynden, at about the same time as Tim and Jessie. We all kind of looked at each other and assured ourselves that this is something we would get through together.

For the remaining eight miles, I found myself driving pretty slowly. I always drive faster than I need to, but not this evening. As each mile went by my heart pumped faster, my left leg shook harder, and my grip on the steering wheel became tighter.

We drove up to the funeral home and I just sat there for a few moments before I could move. I was about to face people who were my family, yet I did not know any one of them. I was about to face my father, the man that I hadn't seen since the day I had pleaded with him not to leave.

I took a few deep breaths, got out of the car and decided to just go on in and not think about it any longer. We were all pretty nervous and nobody moved until I took the lead. Within a moment, I opened the door of the funeral home and walked in.

Of course, nobody knew who we were and I felt as if all eyes were on us. We hung up our coats, walked up the two steps into the main area and kind of stood there in a group.

I had no idea who any of these people were, and I am sure they were thinking the same thing.

My Aunt Margaret, my father's sister, recognized Nathan and came over. She had seen Jessica and Tim a few years back and also recognized them. However, none of them had ever seen me or my family, and once Margaret realized who we all were, she called Grandma Dean over and the introductions began. Within a few moments we were surrounded by relatives; one man—specifically my father—came over, said "Hello" and disappeared into the background.

A whole floodgate of emotions overcame grandma. She started to cry, my two aunts started to cry, and I just kind of stood there stoically. I didn't know what to think; I had always been told how terrible these people were and here it was the most loving reception I have ever had in my life. Grandma just kept on going from one of us kids to the next, hugging us as she went. When she got to the end of the line she started over again. She just could not get over the fact that we were all there.

I asked to see grandpa and grandma grabbed my hand and took me up to the coffin. I looked down at him and was suddenly overcome by an extreme sense of loss. I asked how he had died and learned that he'd had Alzheimer's for the past few years and then pneumonia. She told me what a wonderful man he had been and about his sense of humor, his big heart and how he would have done anything to be involved in my life.

Her arm was around me the entire time as she shared how he agonized over the fact that he was not allowed to know the four of us. They only had seven grandchildren, and when you take away four, it makes quite a dent. I didn't know what to say and just stood there silently while she talked.

There were more relatives lined up to meet us and it was kind of a whirlwind. Everyone we met started to cry and gave us bear hugs. My relatives, no matter how distant, were thrilled to see us. I was told how many prayers had been said asking for this opportunity. I was told over and over again how much my grandfather had loved all of us and how sad it was he couldn't have been a part of our lives.

The inevitable couldn't be avoided any longer. It was time to talk to my father. I grabbed my family, my brothers and sister, and walked towards him. After we exchanged greetings, he suggested that we all go into a side room of the building to visit for a while. It sounded like a good idea and we followed him, sat down and looked at each other rather inquisitively.

His wife was sitting next to him, and his two step-daughters were standing behind him. Needless to say, this reunion was not as emotional as the one with the other relatives. I suppose dad was in shock that we were all there and, speaking only for myself, my guard was up about as high as it could be.

Because my brothers and sister had seen dad in previous years, they were able to pick up a conversation rather easily and were probably not as guarded as I was. I didn't know anything about him, only what I had heard over the years, which was never positive, and I was determined to make light of our visit. I pretty much kept my distance. When dad did ask me a question, I answered in as few words as possible.

About 8:00 we decided that we better head back home. I am not sure which was more difficult that evening, meeting and greeting the people, or trying to figure out how to say good-bye. My mind was swimming with thoughts about the future and wondering what would happen in the days ahead.

I started the good-byes with my father and we shook hands. He took our phone numbers and addresses and said he would be in touch. As he made that statement, I gave him a questioning look. After all, what else is he going to say at a time like this?

While we made our rounds, to say good-bye, there were more hugs and tears from the members of my dad's family, who in point of fact, were my family too. Personally, I didn't shed a tear the entire evening. I had built myself up pretty good for this event and was not going to show the turmoil I felt.

We were asked if we were coming back the next day for the funeral, and if we wanted to stay overnight at my aunt's home, and we declined. Quite honestly, I had never even given that a thought. I don't think I could have taken much more than I had already experienced that evening.

As I put on my coat, bundled up Jeremy and headed out the door, I knew I had done the right thing by coming to this. However, I also knew that I had opened a sore spot in my heart that needed some healing. My intuition was telling me that a painful process was about to begin and that dealing with what I had just opened up was going to be difficult, yet I felt empowered by all of it.

It was a quiet ride home. Pat drove, and I was immersed in my thoughts. My guard was starting to come down, but there were still no tears. I thought about how I hadn't at first recognized any of the people I just met. I thought about how I could have walked by my father on the street, and never had realized it was him. I thought about the heartache my grandparents must have experienced from not being able to know all of their grandchildren. I thought about the times they tried to visit, about the time I saw grandma in the fabric store, and about how different these people were from what I had been told about them throughout my life.

Within a week I received a card from grandma. I think we all did, yet it was never discussed among us. It stated how much it meant to her that I had come to grandpa's visitation and unequivocally how much they both loved us. I was literally shaking, once again, as I read it and re-read it a second time. She included her phone number and requested that I contact her. I was so frightened of everything that I was feeling that I just put the card away. I didn't respond.

I also started receiving newsletters from my father's church; he has been a pastor since about 1985. When I received the generic newsletter, I was angry. I took it as an insult rather than an attempt to be in touch. From then on I received them monthly, but there was no personalization of any kind. I don't think he knew what to do to foster a relationship, and I certainly had no idea how to proceed. However, I did know that I wanted to be more than a name on his church mailing list.

At Easter time we received a big box of items from my father, which included an Easter basket and various toys. Actually, it came from his church. Inside the box, on top of the package, was a note that said "To Peggy's son." That just infuriated me. It said nothing else, and the return address was the church name and street address. It did not say "from dad" or "from grandpa" or anything else.

Things were going well in our lives; we had just bought a house, my career was thriving, and I decided that I didn't want "this" in my world. I wrote dad a letter telling him that I didn't want to receive his newsletters and told him why: if this was his way of justifying staying in touch, I would rather he didn't. I have a tendency to be candid, and I was probably too harsh with him at this point because that was the end of any efforts to communicate for some time, by either one of us. The newsletters stopped and that seemed to be the end of it.

By this time my siblings and I were leading very different lives. We rarely spoke to each other and when we did, it was never about our new-found relatives. I knew that they had had opportunities to forge a relationship with all of these people and for some reason had chosen not to pursue it. They had always known how I felt and, I suppose, figured it was to remain that way.

I was continuing on my path of personal development. I had opened my heart to God's love and decided that I could trust Him. I opened my mind to adopting a new positive attitude about life. I opened my mind to the fact that I needed to "deal" with the events of my past no matter how painful it might be.

Chapter Twenty-Four

Around Christmas in 1994, ten months after I met my Grandma Dean, I had a compulsion to call her. It had been percolating into my consciousness for a few days and I had tried to ignore it. I couldn't rid myself of it, however, so I decided to try to call her. I went to my desk and pulled out the card she had mailed to me after Grandpa Dean's funeral. I knew right where it was, opened it and read it one more time.

I looked at my phone and really debated whether to make that call. I decided now or never, took a deep breath, picked up the phone, dialed her number and was consciously hoping that she wouldn't be there to answer it. That way I could say I had tried but couldn't connect. After two rings she answered. I silently gasped to myself and thought, now what? I had no idea what to say to her, but I knew I had to at least say hello. I asked if Anne was there and she said, "This is she." I said, "This is your granddaughter Peggy." Her hearing wasn't that great and she asked "Who?" So I repeated, "This is your granddaughter Peggy."

Well, she took it from there. She was absolutely thrilled to hear from me. I could feel her smile through the telephone line. We talked for a few minutes—about what I don't recall—and it felt great. My memory of it today *still* feels great. After a few minutes, for fear of running out of things to talk about, I told her I had to get going. Before we said good-bye to one another she stated that my family and I were welcome to come and visit her any time. I thanked her for that but didn't respond.

After I hung up is when the tears finally came. I hadn't shed a tear since I met them almost a year ago, and now, after that conversation they were flowing freely. I was frightened; I didn't want to be hurt, and I was confused because of my upbringing. How could they be so different from everything I had heard? I was always told these people were evil, yet when I talked to Grandma Dean I felt a tremendous outpouring of love from her and I just wanted to reciprocate it.

Three days after that phone conversation I received a letter in the mail. It was from my cousin Sarah. She lived just outside of Lynden, had her own family, was a couple of years older than I and wanted to introduce herself. All of my father's immediate family live in the

Lynden area. Naturally, Grandma Dean told all of them that I had called. Sarah is a first cousin of mine and had asked grandma if she thought it was appropriate to write to me. I am glad that grandma encouraged her to contact me.

As I opened her letter and read it, I shed more tears. I wrote back to her immediately. My response was in the mail the next day with information about my current life, Jeremy and his activities, and my husband. Her letter must have been the push that I needed. It was so welcoming, and accepting, that I decided to call Grandma Dean back and ask if we could come down and visit her on New Year's Day.

It was January 1, 1995 and we were back on Highway 12 heading to Lynden. This time, it was just Pat, Jeremy and I. I did not let my brothers and sister know about this visit. This had to be my venture alone, not ours as a group. It was another nervous drive down. Once again, I couldn't eat much the day before we left, and I hadn't been too productive with my time. This was an all-consuming event for me. My intention was to meet these people with an open mind and forget everything that I had been told. I wanted to make my own judgments and conclusions.

We drove to Grandma Dean's apartment to eat dinner with her that noon. My Aunt Margaret and her husband, Bill, were there also. From the moment we knocked on the door we were showered with love. Grandma and Margaret cried happy tears. I kept it light. We discussed our lives with each other, although I didn't ask any questions about the past or my father. I just wanted to take this all in and to take it slowly. After dinner, we went out to Sarah's home. It was on the same land as Margaret and Bill's farm. Sarah's brother, my cousin Dave, was going to stop by later. My Aunt Joanne, her husband Gary and son Ryan were at Sarah's when we arrived.

This was another welcoming environment; they made every effort to make us feel comfortable. We sat and watched football and had a pleasant visit with each other. I seemed to fit in with these people instantly. My stomach was in knots, and yet I was told later on that I had appeared to be very comfortable. I must have put on a good front, because I was a jumble of emotions on the inside. As we packed up to leave there were more hugs and tears and an open invitation to come and visit whenever we would like to.

On my behalf, it was another quiet drive home. Pat liked these guys, Jeremy had fun playing with Sarah's two boys, who were similar in age, and I was still amazed by how welcoming and loving they were. I can't recall ever being received that warmly or being hugged so much by anyone else in my entire lifetime. It was hard to admit how good it felt.

I'll always remember that day as a turning point in my life. After that visit I wrote a letter to Grandma Dean and my two aunts thanking them for welcoming us into their lives and accepting us for who we were, and for loving us. We continued to correspond throughout that year and visited in person a couple of times. I had to proceed at my own pace, and they allowed me to do that.

Come fall something was happening to me. I found myself feeling angry, from the minute I woke up in the morning until my eyes closed at night. I just felt this negative emotion welling up inside of me. I couldn't control it. I was consistently grouchy towards my family and friends. I am not known for being a particularly patient person, but my impatience seemed to be growing. I found myself feeling envy towards anyone who was happy. I found myself being jealous of people who came from "good" families. I found myself carrying around this heavily burdensome emotion—anger—that I didn't want.

Recognition, or awareness, that there's a problem is the first step to improvement. I have discovered that the only way I can improve myself is to first become aware of my current situation and accept it for what it is. Whether by keeping a journal, spending time in reflection or finding someone who'll talk with us about our unpleasant character traits, it is imperative that we take the time to discover what is at the root of our emotions.

I didn't want to live my life filled with anger. I had been there before and knew how it can destroy any chance for further success or happiness. I had learned that I could control my attitude each and every morning but, I could not control this—no matter how many times I told myself I could.

My anger started affecting my performance with my clients and my relationships at home. Within a couple of weeks I decided to get some help. This was bigger than what I knew how to solve and I decided to talk to a professional and try and figure out why I was so angry. After all, I had a new family that embraced me to my core. Things were going well in my real estate career, and I was finally experiencing some of the benefits of my hard work. My husband and I were becoming closer every day. My son was thriving, I liked my home and it's neighborhood. My life was good, what did I have to be so angry about?

I made an appointment to see a counselor at my church on November 1, 1995. Her name was Marty, and in order for her to be of any help to me, I had to share my life story with her. I had not done that with anyone in my church, or around town, prior to this meeting. I was pretty apprehensive about it, but I knew I didn't have a choice.

In fact, Marty was pretty surprised when I called her for help. I had been an active volunteer within the church, and nobody really knew anything about me. I had wanted it that way and had never shown any inkling that I was going through some difficult times.

That afternoon, sitting in the church's library, I opened up and shared my life's trials publicly, for the first time. It was tough sharing things that I had buried deep within my soul, and I found myself literally shaking as I began.

Marty was a great listener and by the time our visit was concluded I felt somewhat liberated. Confused, but liberated. I headed on home and decided to just take it easy the rest of the day. As the afternoon wore on, I was feeling a variety of emotions, but the main one was relief—relief that I was finally going to deal with everything bad that had happened in my life. I wasn't actually looking forward to the process, of course; I was looking forward to the end result of being a happy person and enjoying life to its fullest.

After all those years, I was finally ready to surrender my stubborn will and do what was needed to free myself of my "baggage." It all starts with the desire to change, and the desire was finally there.

Two days after my visit with Marty I had an insight that resulted from my writing down my thoughts in a journal. I had just received notice that mom and Grandpa and Grandma Baker were coming up for a visit that following weekend. They were coming up on Sunday morning and I was to drive them to Stillwater to visit grandma's niece, Betty, and her family for the afternoon. They would then spend the night at a hotel in Hastings, and we would have breakfast together Monday morning before they headed back home.

On receiving this phone call I instantly felt annoyed. I was frustrated and couldn't quite put my finger on it, but when I sat down and wrote out my thoughts, I discovered the source of my anger: I was angry with my mom and my grandparents for keeping me away from my dad's family, for the way they had treated that other side of my family all these years, and for all that I had been deprived of while I was growing up.

Now I had something that I could work with. That weekend, when they came for their visit, I was caught up in a whirlwind of emotions. My feelings varied from happiness at seeing them and wishing I could spend more time with them, to anger for all the "lost" years, to guilt for feeling the way I did about them at times, and to sadness due to the reality of our relationship.

On top of that, when we went to visit Betty, I also found myself feeling envious. Her two daughters stopped in and the three of them seemed to be very close and were sharing some of the good times they had together.

Sitting there listening to them laugh and feeling the love between them, I found myself wishing that I had a mother, or grandmother, with whom I could have a relationship like that. I found myself feeling a sense of remorse for what I didn't have.

Within moments, however, I found myself feeling hope and excitement, because maybe I *had* found someone to have a relationship like that with in Grandma Dean, and yet that scared me. What if I was getting my hopes up too high? What if she didn't really want me in her world? What if she wouldn't accept me?

I was happy, in many ways, when it was time to head back to Hastings that Sunday afternoon. I needed some time alone with my thoughts and some encouragement to continue on this path of self-improvement. While we were driving back home it dawned on me that I didn't even know how to relate to close family relationships. The families that I had known had done nothing but hurt me.

That following Monday morning I wanted to stay in bed and never crawl out. My head was just swimming with thoughts; I had no idea there were all of these pent-up feelings inside of me, and when I grabbed pen and paper they just started pouring out of me. It finally dawned on me why I had behaved the way I had over the years—I had had no guidance or positive role models and was left to figure things out on my own.

Maybe things would have turned out differently if somebody had come to me and offered guidance and love (without other motives). But that didn't happen and, as Marty suggested to me that afternoon during our second meeting, I needed to forgive the people in my world at whom I was angry.

I felt like I wanted to fall off my chair when she said that to me. I could not believe that she was telling me I needed to forgive the people who had hurt me. How did she expect me to do that and why would I want to? To top that off she even went so far as to tell me that I needed to write a letter to my father.

She could tell what I was thinking without my saying a word and was very good about throwing the suggestion out there and letting me decide when, and if, to proceed. My first reaction was to decline her advice. It is human nature to judge things that are brought our way and to dismiss some things before we have even tried them. I am simply human and decided to ignore that one for a few days.

The good news, though, is that I only ignored it for about a week, and on November 15, 1995 I sat down and wrote out 10 pages of events that I needed to put behind me, people who I needed to forgive, and mistakes that I needed to take responsibility for. If I were to stay angry, it would only keep affecting me, and I didn't want to continue down that road.

The greatest example I have of what sustained anger does to a person is my mother. The anger that she has carried around has ruined her life. In essence, it ruined our childhood. Ironically, it didn't affect the people that she was angry at; it only affected her.

That day gave me a wonderful feeling of freedom. I don't think I can even quite verbalize how it feels to get all that "baggage" off your back and, by doing so, to allow yourself to move ahead in a positive direction. I am not naïve enough to believe that it only takes one time through this process and everything is fixed. There are still moments today when I need to remind myself that I have already forgiven that person, or issue, from my past. The thing is, it is important to start the process. Write it down as many times as you need to, as many days in a row as are necessary, until you feel that freedom that I realized.

It is reported that it takes 21 days for the average person to create a habit. The idea here is that we are creating a habit of forgiveness rather than holding on to things that will only hold us back. It is like a cleansing of the soul. As a Christian, the Scriptures tell me that the Lord will forgive me for my sins so long as I ask with a clear heart.

In the realm of life, that is all that matters. If the Lord can forgive us, then we certainly ought to be able to forgive ourselves. When people ask me how I have become what I have today or how I changed the road that I had started down, I tell them that forgiveness has been a crucial factor. It was one of the most difficult steps I had to take, yet very well worth it. I had a lot of issues to forgive, a lot of tears to shed, and a lot of pride to set aside. But, I would have never found inner happiness without that process.

As the saying goes "When the student is ready the teacher will appear." That rang true in my situation. Even though Marty and I only met two other times, she was the teacher and I was the student. In fact, many of us have experienced moments when we hear something we need to hear, see something we need to see and think something we need to think.

When the time is right, things that are supposed to happen, will. Some of the most difficult and trying situations in our lives result from our trying to force things to happen that aren't yet meant to be. That doesn't mean, of course, that we should just sit back and wait for life to happen. I am suggesting that we must do whatever is humanly possible on our own behalf, and trust the process for the rest of it.

Right before the 1995 holiday season I did sit down and write my father a letter. This one was not as harsh as the previous one; rather, it was more of an attempt to find out what I needed to learn from him. I opened my heart by sharing with him where I was with all of my "stuff," asked him several questions about his life, and stated my desire and need to hear from him.

As I sent the letter off, I tried not to get my hopes up too high, but I would be lying if I pretended that I wasn't disappointed when he didn't respond. I didn't expect an immediate reply, but I was quite confused when months had gone by without a word from him.

On the brighter side, my relationship with the rest of dad's side of the family continued to blossom. It was, and is, a true blessing in my life. My Grandmother Dean and I grew incredibly close; I found the kind of close relationship with her that I had hoped for.

Grandma Dean would become almost giddy when we visited with her. Half the excitement of going to see her was simply watching how happy it made her. She had been praying for 22 years that she would have the chance to know her "other" grandkids. Well, she didn't get to know all of them, but the one she did know became very special to her.

Getting to know my relatives on my father's side has given me the family that I was always looking for. As our relationship grew I found the courage to begin to ask more questions about my father and the cause of his leaving us when I was a child.

We also discovered that when I was 18 years old and living in Fairview, I was within eight miles of my grandparents and other relatives, and none of us knew it. Grandpa and Grandma Dean used to come in and eat quite often at the restaurant where I worked. We wondered if we ever ran into each other inadvertently. It amazed each and every one of us how close in proximity we had been at various times in our lives without crossing paths.

There are still times that I feel regret for all the pain and anguish that resulted from the rift between my mom and the Dean family. I truly could have used their love and support throughout my youth and childhood, but I have come to accept the fact that I need to be thankful for what I have now without worrying about what I didn't have as a child or young adult.

I don't know how I made it without the love and support of these people all those years, but we have all made a mutual agreement to forgive the past and make the most out of the present.

In December 1995, Grandpa Baker passed away. It happened unexpectedly. I received a phone call from Nathan one morning at about 8:00 A.M. He said he had just gotten off the phone with mom and that grandpa was in the hospital, dying.

Knowing that Nathan tends to exaggerate things, I didn't believe him. After all, I had just seen grandpa a few days ago to celebrate my niece's birthday and he was perfectly healthy. I took some pictures of him playing with his great grandkids and being the comic relief that he always was in our family.

I just could not believe what Nathan was telling me—that our grandpa was dying. I thought it possible that he was in the hospital, but not dying. I figured it was just mom over-reacting to the situation. She tends to do that and I have learned that I can't always believe exactly what she tells me.

Nathan tends to have some of those same characteristics. He gets upset very easily, and I know that my ambivalence did not help the situation. I told him that I would call the hospital in Deerborne and find out for myself what was happening and that I would get right back to him.

Once I was connected to grandpa's room, I could tell by the tone of Aunt Edith's voice that something serious was going on. She sounded pretty upset and I asked her if what mom had said was true. She confirmed it and suggested that I get down there as soon as I could. I was in a bit of shock. How could this be? He seemed perfectly healthy just three days ago, and now he was dying.

I quickly called Nathan back to let him know what I had learned, and I was out of the house within a half hour of hearing the news. Grandpa had experienced a brain aneurysm and could go at any moment. I jumped in my car, made that 60-mile drive as fast as I could and was at the hospital by 9:15 A.M.

As I walked into his room, it was pretty clear to me that Grandpa Baker didn't have long to live. It was a surreal experience; I held his hand and talked to him for a moment, but there was no response. He was just lying there with his eyes closed; his breathing was labored.

The room was filling up with his grandkids and before long a nurse came in and asked us all to leave for a few moments. She wanted some privacy to check some vital signs on grandpa and we begrudgingly headed out the door. Just as the last of us were leaving the room, the nurse frantically called us back in; grandpa was dying.

We all rushed back in and allowed room for mom, grandma and Edith to stand around his bed. Mom stood rather apathetically at the side of the bed, crying; Edith was hugging grandpa, almost half-laying on him, crying and telling him over and over that she loved him, grandma stood on the other side of the bed and held his hand.

I kind of stood in the background, not knowing what to do, yet not wanting to leave either. I was watching grandma, as grandpa was passing away, trying to figure out how I would be reacting if this were Pat on the hospital bed. Grandma stood there, anxiously repeating over and over again, "I just can't believe this; Edward don't leave me, don't leave me."

Right before grandpa took his last breath, Edith was saying, almost pleadingly, "Mom, tell dad you love him." Edith kept telling grandma to let grandpa know that she loved him, but, grandma never did. Grandpa passed away without hearing the words "I love you" from his wife.

I will never forget that moment. I could not believe that my grandma could not tell my grandpa, as he was dying, that she loved him. To this day, I still shake my head in amazement over that. They had spent 60 years together as husband and wife. What prevented grandma from making that statement? I doubt I will ever know.

~

I stayed with grandma that first night, so she wouldn't be alone. I had thrown a few extra clothes in my car before I left home, just in case I needed them. I wanted to stay and help grandma however I could. I really do love my grandma; even though we haven't always seen eye-to-eye, there is still a strong bond between us.

Grandma didn't sleep much that first night; she spent a lot of it crying, which would be expected. She came out of her room about 5:00 the next morning and just stood and cried in the hallway. I got out of bed, went to her and hugged her. That was an odd sensation for me. I don't think I had ever really hugged her before and I don't recall her hugging me before. Both of us are very strong, independent people. While the hug didn't last too long, I am glad I was there for her.

I didn't shed a tear until three days later, after it was all over: the planning, the visitation, and the funeral. Most of my family members were distraught and I found myself taking the "strong lead" once again. Even though I had been working through the emotions of meeting my dad's side of the family, and had now lost the person who had been the father figure my entire life, I still found myself taking care of the people around me.

I guess I have come to accept that I am the care-taker for my family, and I am OK with that. I fought it for quite a few years, but the fact is, I am the one who is best equipped to fulfill that role. We all have roles to play in our families. Sometimes we don't like the role we're given, but the way I see it, somebody had to be strong for the rest of my family and I seemed to be the most qualified.

Grandpa's funeral was an awakening for me. I heard my cousins share stories about all their good memories and the good times they had with him. It was odd, because our family didn't have those same stories even though, over the years, we had spent more time with him. It seemed like my cousins knew a different person, a different grandpa, than the one I knew. I suppose he was able to truly be "just a grandpa" to them.

It was not until I was in my car that I allowed myself to grieve. I didn't drive as fast this time and actually found myself going at an easy pace. It seems that I gain my strength from my private time. I use it in reflection and prayer to God for perseverance and courage.

Chapter Twenty-Five

The holidays came and went and we began another year. My real estate career was thriving and yet, as always, it wasn't enough. I was getting bored with it and was looking for more. I began doing some local training for agents in my office and discovered that I really enjoyed helping other people. I was told, on several occasions that I had a natural talent for this kind of thing. It seemed that I had a passion for sharing what I had learned and decided to take it a step further.

In April 1996 I met with the Director of Training for the real estate company I had been working with and told him I wanted to become a part of his training staff for our company's new agents. He gave me a list of items to be completed before that could happen and I acted on them immediately. That May I gave my first presentation and was added to the schedule on a monthly basis. Without consciously realizing it, my life was changing, again. This time, though, it was for the better.

It is astonishing how quickly old characteristics and personality traits—traits that one thought were long since conquered—can resurface. May 21, 1996, I received a call from Grandma Baker. While grandpa was still alive they had asked me if I would like to, someday, have their set of china for my home. Naturally, I said yes and was thrilled that they wanted to give a cherished piece of their life to me, something to which lots of memories from holidays past and family celebrations were attached.

After grandpa's funeral, we sold quite a bit of their things at an auction and moved grandma into a smaller home. She didn't have room for the china and was calling me that day to ask if I still wanted it. Naturally I said yes, and she then went on to tell me that I would have to pay $900 for it. I was surprised and didn't really know what to say. Grandma went on to explain that she had had the china appraised recently for $1500 and felt that $900 was a fair asking price.

My heart sank and my blood pressure rose. My own grandma wanted to charge me for something that she and grandpa had planned on giving to me. I was so angry that I couldn't even speak to her.

When I did find the gumption to say something, the only thing that came out of my mouth was, "I will have to talk to Pat." With that we bid good-bye and I hung up the phone.

I was just fuming, mainly because I hadn't even had the nerve to say no to her. There was no way we were going to spend that kind of money on a set of china. Sure, it would have been nice to have, but it wasn't something that I would have spent money on. To top that off, I started to feel guilty about not buying it and that made me even more angry. Why should I feel guilty about saying no to her?

Fortunately, I had learned how to deal with my anger much earlier. I knew I had to forgive the event by writing it down and repeating to myself, "I forgive grandma for asking me to buy her china." The key in this life management thing is to recognize the sources of our stress and resolve them as quickly as we can. Where we get into trouble is when we avoid that practice.

Chapter Twenty-Six

On August 30, 1996 I received another momentous phone call. This time it was John. John from Oregon. Another shocker of a phone call.

It had been five years since I had last seen or heard from him. I don't know how he knew my married name or where to find me, but somehow he tracked me down. He was in Fargo, North Dakota and was going to be in Minneapolis the next day for a lay-over and wanted to see me and Jeremy.

John had been straight, and sober, for well over a year and he was making his amends. Without giving it much thought, I agreed to meet him. I talked it over with Pat and he didn't like it, but he understood my need for closure. I had a lot of issues to deal with, and it seemed that the Lord just kept bringing them my way. The Bible says that He will not give us more than we can handle, but sometimes I really question His judgment.

While it was rather uncomfortable to see John, I am glad I went. He was doing well and that was nice to see. John apologized for everything he had done to "us" and I accepted the apology. John had been part of my forgiveness process some time back. However, seeing him brought back many of the feelings and emotions that I had kept hidden away since moving back to Minnesota.

Good things came out of our meeting, though. I realized that I would not be as happy as I am today if I had not gone through what I did with John. Seeing someone from your past can create all sorts of "what-if" thoughts, and I found myself going down that path. What if John hadn't relapsed? What if I hadn't moved back to Minnesota?

I went home that day and spent the rest of the afternoon and evening in my bedroom, crying. I was shedding some tears that I hadn't allowed myself to shed previously but it was time to grieve and move on. Thankfully, Pat and Jeremy respected my space.

When I woke up the next morning I felt empowered again. I knew that my life was on the right track and that I had done the right thing by moving back here with my son. I also realized that "what ifs" have no relevance in our world. It is a waste of time and energy to regret things from our past. If we can use that time to learn from them, well and good. But if we use the past as a club with which to beat ourselves, well...we should refuse to go that route.

I had set for myself the goal of becoming the training director of the real estate company I was working with for 1997. The current director, who had hired me, was being promoted and moving to Chicago. I felt I was up for the job and communicated and demonstrated my confidence. In February I received the promotion.

I was excited to achieve this. It meant giving up my sales career, but that was all right by me. It seemed that I had finally discovered an outlet for my energy and drive.

Three months later, however, I was miserable. I had thought that this was the spot for me. I realized, to my disappointment, that I had been an independent contractor too long and really did not like being an employee and involved in corporate life. I have nothing against the corporate professions; to each their own. I just found that I dreaded the limitations it offered. Now what was I going to do? I had worked hard to get here, had given up my sales career and had adjusted our family life to my commuting and working Monday through Friday from 8:00 A.M. to 6:00 P.M.

Well, as always, we have options. We can choose to stay where we are and be miserable, or we can charge ahead. I chose the latter. In August 1997 I incorporated my own business and was set to give my resignation at the end of that year. I had decided to take a risk and become a professional speaker/author. It was something I would never have thought possible only three years ago, something that I could never have imagined myself doing. The thought of it was so exciting that I couldn't even sit down.

There are lots of challenges in creating and forming your own business. That is for another book. The interesting thing is, though, that my journal entry for February 12, 1998 says the following:

"Things are happening for me. I am continuing to improve myself each and every day. I am having small successes with my business, which will lead to bigger ones. I feel incredibly at peace with what is happening in my life. However, there are still some unresolved issues to take care of, mainly, my father. I have been looking for answers as to why my father and I haven't connected and why he has never replied to that

letter I sent a couple of years ago. My life has become more than I had ever expected, yet I haven't completely dealt with 'I got' and I don't know how to make that happen."

Apparently, God had a plan.

~~~

On February 14th, 1998 my Uncle Bill passed away. He was the uncle that I had just met a couple of years earlier, my father's brother-in-law. He had been diagnosed with cancer and was gone within a year. For Bill, it was a blessing that his suffering had ended. For us, it was a different story.

Bill's death was pretty hard on me. I think there were too many things going on all at once. I am confident there was a reason for all of it, but that doesn't mean I had to like it. My greatest fear, at the moment of Bill's passing away, was of seeing my father; I was also fearful of *not* seeing my father.

Dad had been home once since Grandpa Dean died and had made no effort to contact me. I found out about his visit after he had already left. Grandma Dean had encouraged him to call me, yet he didn't.

None of us was really sure if dad would come to Bill's funeral. He had been pretty detached from our family since that original move to Missouri. It would have disappointed me enormously if he hadn't shown up, because of my feelings for Aunt Margaret and her family. However, I was also panicked at the thought of him being there.

Margaret knew that it would be challenging for me to see my dad—after all, the last time I saw him hadn't gone all that well. It had taken a lot for me to open up to him and send him that last letter, and it was rather humiliating that he never took the time to reply.

In fact, both grandma and Margaret told me that they would understand if I chose not to attend Bill's visitation, or funeral, or any of it. I couldn't stay away—Bill was a special person in my life—even if it had been for only a few years. I couldn't stay away just because there was a possibility of one person, my dad, showing up.

Two days later, Monday, February 16, the day of the visitation, I was about to face my father, and I felt like a basket case. My emotions were varied and extremely intense. I hadn't a clue as to what to do when I saw him.

Many of my friends and family members had said that I should just ignore him, but I wasn't at all sure that was the answer. The day before, in church, I asked for prayers for Margaret and her two children and their families. I also shared that I would be seeing my father and needed prayers for that. I started to cry, uncontrollably, and could barely get the words out of my mouth. I sat and cried through the entire church service.

That kind of experience is rather odd. People around me didn't know what to say or how to react and when people don't know how to react, they tend to avoid a person. I had rarely showed my emotions, and crying in church was unheard of for me. Crying in front of *anyone* was unheard of. That day, though, I couldn't help it. I couldn't stop crying. I was unbelievably frightened at the prospect of seeing my father, and I suppose all those years of avoiding the confrontation had built a huge pressure inside me. Now the dreaded encounter was right in front of me. I was going to be with him for two days and had no inkling about what to expect.

As I drove up to the funeral home that Monday afternoon I was trying to remain strong and could not figure out why I was so emotional about seeing my dad. After all, I had met him here, in this exact building, four years ago and that hadn't seemed so difficult. Why was this so much harder?

As I parked my car and looked around, I saw a van with license plates from Missouri. That meant my dad was already inside and I just froze. If nothing else, I at least wanted to be there before he was, but that wasn't going to happen. I took a deep breath and was determined to not let him see my feelings. Silly pride.

I said a quick prayer, reminded myself of Philippians 4:13, "I can do all things through Christ which strengthens me" and walked on in. Naturally, he was right by the entrance. I played it cool, hung up my jacket, looked at him and said "Hello." Dad replied by saying "Hey, girl" and I walked on by to find someone, anyone, to talk to.

Within an hour Pat and Jeremy met me at the funeral home. I had come down earlier in the day to be with Margaret and intended to stay overnight. Pat and Jeremy had to head back home later that evening for school and work the next day.

While Pat and Jeremy were there we avoided my father and he avoided us. It was an easy thing to do, with all of the people coming in and out of the visitation. After Pat and Jeremy left, I went and sat in the general vicinity that my father was in. That is where the rest of the family was sitting, and it seemed appropriate. Dad didn't look at me or say a word. I looked at him occasionally, but he never made eye contact with me. I was starting to feel really hurt by this and I said to myself, "No, Peggy, you're above this."

I was sitting next to my Great Uncle Marion, who is a wonderful man with a big heart. I asked him what was wrong with my dad and why he didn't want to talk to me and if I was supposed to make the first move. Marion grabbed my hand, put his other arm around me and said, "Peggy, don't feel bad. Your dad doesn't know what he is missing, and it's up to him to make the first move toward a conversation."

Well, he never made a first move and neither did I. He left without saying anything to me and I let him. I didn't understand why he didn't make any type of effort to speak to me when I was sitting within 10 feet of him. I wished I had been able to look at him and feel something or gain a sense of his feelings, but I couldn't. I didn't want to be hurt anymore by him. I was in agony and felt like he was abandoning me all over again.

That night I stayed at Margaret's. My purpose was simply to be there for her, so she wouldn't be alone. She ended up spending as much time comforting me as I did her. My father was in a local hotel, about five miles from where I was, and neither of us was making any kind of effort to forge a relationship with each other.

I didn't sleep much that night. I was tossing and turning, and turning and tossing. I felt miserable and didn't know what to do about it. I felt a strong sense that this might be my last chance to speak with my father for years to come. I prayed and asked God to give me another opportunity the following day; another opportunity to say more than hello; another opportunity before dad left to go back home, at about 5:00 that next afternoon.

As I was getting ready the next morning, February 17, I was focused on one objective: to talk to my dad that day. I didn't know what I was going to say or how I was going to make that happen. I was just set on receiving something, anything, more from him than a "Hey, girl."

I drove to the church as slowly as I could, to kill time. I parked the car, sat there for a few moments, decided I couldn't delay it any longer, got out of my car and proceeded to walk down the sidewalk and into the main entrance.

There, standing by himself, by the door, was my father. Have you ever heard of the saying, "Be careful what you pray for because you might get it"? Well, I "got it" and wasn't ready for it.

It was the perfect opportunity for me to say something, and nothing came out but "Hello" and a forced smile. He said "Hi" back and said something about having van trouble. I didn't respond; I couldn't say anything to this man and I ended up walking away to speak with other relatives.

Before long, family members were invited downstairs for a private service. By design, I was one of the last people down and wouldn't you know it, there was an empty chair by my dad. It was one of the few empty chairs, and I just decided to stand in back by myself. There was no way I could go and sit by him.

I avoided dad as best I could during both the private family service and the public one upstairs. I sat with grandma for the one upstairs, and my father and his wife ended up sitting right behind us. I knew he was back there, I wanted to turn around and acknowledge him, and I couldn't do it. I couldn't do anything—I felt as if I was paralyzed.

At the completion of the service I got in the car with Uncle Marion, his wife Bergie, and Grandma Dean to head out to the cemetery. As soon as we were all in the car and buckled in, I asked quite anxiously, "Why won't that man talk to me?"

Grandma started to cry, grabbed my hand and stated that she wished she could change things. I said, "Grandma, I don't expect you to change anything. I just don't understand why he doesn't make more of an effort?"

From the driver's seat, Uncle Marion said, quite angrily, "It's his job to break the ice—not yours." With that, the rest of the trip was silent. I believe they wanted to make things better and just didn't know how. I sat there, looking out the window and silently asked, "OK Lord, I know I passed up two opportunities this morning to talk to dad and I only asked for one. Please give me one more?"

We arrived at the cemetery to see dad walking up to the gravesite. Due to the cold weather his wife had chosen to stay in the car. I was a jumble of nerves as Marion parked the car, and I wished that I could just sit there and wait for this day to end. However, I knew that I would be very disappointed in myself if I did.

I opened the door, crawled out into the snow bank, ran to the other side to help grandma out, and walked her up to the service to help her find a chair. As soon as she was settled, I backed away from the main family area and somehow my father and I ended up standing near each other, within about three feet or so, without many other people around. We didn't know what to do or what to say. I looked at him and he looked at me. I tried to read what his eyes were telling me and couldn't. We stood there in silence, neither of us saying a darn thing.

~

Even though the service was short, about 15 minutes, it felt like hours. We started to leave and my father went in front of me. He slipped on the ice and I held my hand out to help. It was an involuntary response and after I did it, I had no idea why I had.

We both stopped and I thought to myself "now or never." I looked him directly in the eyes, we kind of smiled at each other, and I asked, "Hey, are you going to talk to me today?"

He asked, "Do you want me to?" I said, "Yeah, I do. I only want about five to ten minutes to ask you a few questions." He grinned at me once more and agreed, that, yes when we got back to the church for the luncheon, we would talk.

My heart was pounding and felt as though it was racing a million beats a minute. I told grandma, Marion and Bergie what I had said to dad. They were pleased that one of us had finally taken the initiative to open the lines of communication. I had a hard time sitting still for the drive back to the church. My palms were sweaty, my breathing was quick and now my head was pounding. I hadn't the slightest idea what I wanted to say to my father, but the time was upon me to come up with something.

We arrived back at the church before dad and I went and sat by my cousins. They were already eating, but there was no way I could eat anything. My stomach was in knots and I was anxiously awaiting the arrival of my father.

When he did arrive, he got his wife settled and then came directly over to me. He asked me if I wanted to go over to the side of the room so we could have some privacy and I agreed. I got up from my chair and he put his hand on my back to lead the way. Without even thinking about it, I shied away from his touch.

We found an empty table and sat down. Just as we did, the minister of Margaret and Bill's church, came and sat down directly across from dad. I was going crazy inside! Here I finally had a chance to talk to my father and now we were being interrupted.

It was an honest interruption. The Pastor had no idea of the situation and he wanted to talk to another clergyman, who just happened to be my dad. I think we both gave off some pretty strong vibes signaling him to leave, however, because within five minutes he was getting up and looking for another place to sit.

The ten minutes I had asked my dad for turned into 45. I ended up asking him all sorts of questions that just kind of spewed out of me. I wanted to know why he never replied to that last letter I sent him. Why didn't he talk to me last night? Who was he? What goes on in his world? How did it feel to see your little girl all grown up?

I told him I was highly disappointed in both of us for our actions the previous night. He told me about encounters he'd had with my brothers and sister, my mother and her family and seemed to put me in the same category as all of them. He said he felt he should play it cool, wasn't sure how I felt about him and he didn't want to offend me. I explained, quite explicitly, that I am my own person; that I live, think and act differently from my siblings and my mother and her parents.

He went on to say that he doesn't do a very good job of keeping in touch with anyone. I said "So what, I am your daughter." He said, "I live by a time clock." I said, "So does the rest of society; if it were a priority, you'd find the time."

He went on to tell me that he doesn't want to be hurt. I wasn't expecting him to say that, yet it was exactly how I was feeling. The first thought that ran through my mind was "How could I hurt him?" It really kind of threw me off.

I said, "Earl, I don't hold anything against you and I don't care about the past. I am trying to figure out who I am and I need to deal with this so I can move on! The last year of my life I have really struggled with everything that I missed out on as a child. I don't know why it's happening now, but it is. I don't want pity, sympathy or lip service. Please don't say things just to make me feel good."

Of course, I was on a roll and so I said " I can't image the hurt of not knowing your four children, and then seeing your little girl when she is a 30-year-old woman." He replied, "You have no idea," and started to cry.

I just sat and looked at him. I was not expecting this from this person who is my father. It had never occurred to me that he, too, had been hurt by this entire situation. We talked a little more about our current lives and I felt that I had said everything that I needed to say to him at that point. It was time for me to be heading back home and I told him thanks for his time. He told me that he cared for me and that I have a spot in his heart. I didn't reply.

We walked over towards the rest of the family and I said my good-byes. I didn't actually say good-bye to my father. He had gone to sit with his wife and I had had enough for the day. On the drive home I was a bundle of emotions. I felt very unsure about him. I didn't want to be disappointed, felt incredibly vulnerable and yet, for some reason, I also felt a tremendous amount of love for him.

~

The next morning, after a restless night, I wrote my father a letter. Here are pieces of what I wrote to him:

February 18, 1998
Hi Earl! You have really been on my mind since I talked

with you. Thank you for taking the time to listen to me and answer a couple of questions (as much as you could).

I don't know what to think about anything right now. I do know that I need to communicate with you. I have worked really hard to overcome everything from my past. As I said to you, I have worked on many levels of "stuff" and I think I am now at the level of needing to know you. I hope you do not deny me this because of other commitments in your life.

*I got the impression when I was talking with you that you have experienced a lot of hurt and pain also. It never occurred to me that our separation hurt you just as much as, if not more than, me. I don't know why that never occurred to me before. I suppose I just thought you were oblivious to it all since I haven't received any kind of response from you. As I shared with you, Earl, I don't hold **anything** against you. I have no reason to.*

Right now my heart is saying one thing and my head is telling me something different. It is emotion versus logic. The emotional side of me wants to know my dad. The little girl in me needs to know I am loved by you. The adult in me says don't get your hopes up, don't fabricate anything, don't expect anything—just stay away. The emotional side of me says I have to try. You see, through a lot of painful growth I have discovered that I have this tremendous need for approval from people in my life. I think I now know why—I need approval and acceptance from you that I was never able to receive.

With the help of God I have become a new person. I am proud of who I am and what I am all about. It took me up until the last two years to be able to say that and believe it. I believe there is a reason for everything that has happened to me in my life, and I believe that reason is to help others learn about overcoming obstacles and what life is all about. I am living proof that anyone can overcome anything—if they want to badly enough.

When I saw Bill in his coffin I thought about how tragic it would be if that were you and I had never taken an opportunity or made an effort to know you. I met my Grandpa Dean at his funeral four years ago, and that was an awful experience. I don't ever want that to happen again with anyone in my life

Again, Earl, I don't want to push you into anything or make you uncomfortable. I am not looking to replace anyone or anything in your life. I just want to know who my dad is. Please take the time to contact me, or write back. Please don't let the past hinder you from knowing me. I am not looking to go back and make things better. I am looking for a more fulfilling future.

Dad came into my life when I was ready for it. If I had met him even five years earlier, I am confident nothing would have come of it. I am confident that I would not have been able to deal with the situation as maturely as I did when we finally did meet. This was just the beginning, yet I felt sure this was something I had to do. I had to get to know my father. How else would I be able to truly know who I am? How else would I be able to truly move on to better things in my world if I didn't at least try to put the pieces of my puzzle together? I needed to create some healing for my soul, and I would not be complete unless I did whatever was humanly possible to overcome this hurdle that my father represented.

After I wrote the letter and sent it off in the mail, I found myself really nervous. I had no idea how he was going to react to our visit, to my letter or anything at all about me. I didn't even know if he wanted to know who I was, or if he was interested at all in my life. After all, he didn't appear overly anxious to resolve or create anything between us. He is a hard person to read. Funny thing, I have been told the same about myself.

A few days went by and I hadn't heard anything yet. I reasoned with myself by saying it takes a few days for the mail to get a letter to Missouri and he probably needed time to think things over. Just because I act on my decisions immediately does not mean that everyone else does.

I was talking over the situation with a friend, and she told me not to get my hopes up. She said my dad may not be interested in me, and maybe he moved on years ago. I didn't like to hear that. I tend to think more positively. I could have sat and worried over her bit of "wisdom," but I have learned that I can't worry about things until they're truly in front of me. I am not sure how I would have reacted if I had never received a reply. Thankfully, I never had to go down that street.

On February 25, 1998, I received a response. Dad faxed me a quick note acknowledging my letter and stating that he would send more when he had a moment to do it. I was elated when I received that fax!

In fact, the way I felt scared me. I had no idea that this was so important to me. I had no idea that a simple little one-page fax from my father could make me feel like I was on top of the world. I was so happy I cried. I seem to have spent a lot of time crying during those past few months and years; it had never been like me to do, yet I always felt better after I did.

~

Another emotion was coming on strong at this time. It is called the "fear of success," the feeling that one isn't worthy of the good things in one's life.

This really stood out when it came time for me to hire someone to help me with the marketing of my programs. I needed to find someone to help me prospect and get the word out about my message. I talked to everyone I knew for names of people who could fill this role.

Within a few days I had compiled a list of four candidates. Three were people whom I already knew, people who probably were not the best candidates. One, Kathy, was a sister of my sister-in-law's friend. I had no idea who she was, but when I looked at her name on the list I became nervous. If I were to call her, and she were good, then I would really have to step up to the plate and prove that I can do this.

In any case, I went the easy route and found someone who I knew through the real estate business. We worked together for two weeks and it didn't work out. She was going through some personal challenges; facing a divorce and with kids to feed, she had to take a full-time job to make ends meet.

It didn't surprise me that this happened. Upon reflection, I can clearly see that I unconsciously called a person to work with me who was not necessarily the best fit for me. It was my way of avoiding really stepping up to the plate in my career. It was my way of avoiding success. I was afraid of what success might bring my way and I still deal with this on many levels.

If I were to hire Kathy, and things went well, then my life would change. I would have to be able to deal with the responsibilities that success can bring. It would mean more personal growth, overcoming more obstacles and paving a path that had an undetermined end result. What if I couldn't make my new career work? Who did I think I was to be going out and talking to people about improving life? Look where I came from, who am I kidding? Yes, if Kathy came to work for me I would not be able to "hide" behind anything anymore.

~

On March 4, 1998, I went to the gym early in the morning to exercise. I do this a few times a week for my stress relief. I leave feeling more self-confident about things in my world.

When I got home, I went through my ritual of checking our home answering machine, my business voice mail, and my fax machine. I received a touching two-page letter from my dad and was literally shaking (once again) as I read it. I sat and cried and cried and cried until there were no more tears. He said he was proud of me and he wanted to get to know me.

Dad also shared some memories of us being together when I was young. I was simultaneously happy and more frightened than ever. I was afraid of being hurt, but this time I decided to not let that get in the way. I could miss out on a beautiful relationship if I chose to hide behind the walls I had built around my heart. We could really miss out on lots of wonderful things in our world due to our fear of being hurt. I was at a point in my life where the potential benefit was more than worth the risk. I could not let this opportunity go by.

Within a few days of receiving that letter I wrote back. Questions were just pouring out of me. The amazing thing was that I don't remember ever having been that curious about him or his life or what happened between my parents—until that moment. I truly had had no awareness of how much I loved my dad, or what that relationship had meant to me as a child—until then.

I was also discovering some things about myself on this venture. I look at my son and see how sensitive he is, and I wonder if I was like that at one point in my life. I see how much my son needs my attention on a daily basis, and I wonder how I survived after my father left, my stepfather left, and the separation from the rest of my family? I wonder if I was as positive about life as Jeremy is?

I see my son and all the potential he has in this world, and I wonder what things may have been like for me if I'd had a supportive person in my life; someone to encourage me and believe in me.

The end of that month came and I decided to take the plunge and call Kathy to see if she was still interested in working with me. I felt as if my confidence was growing on a daily basis; it seemed as if my life was changing right before my eyes.

On the last Saturday of the month, March 28, I stayed in bed until 2:30 P.M. When I awoke that morning I had no energy, no drive, no nothing. I just needed to sleep. I believe the events of the previous couple of months had taken their toll. I needed to care for my soul and the way to do that was to allow myself a day to do nothing, worry about nothing and pamper myself.

Years ago I would have never allowed myself to relax for a day like this. It is important that we grant ourselves time—and give ourselves permission—to heal our wounds. This was a day that I could do that. I have found that when I spend time in bed it is like re-energizing myself for life. I spend it in prayer, visioning, reflecting and just simply doing nothing. By 4:00 that afternoon, I was ready to get back to dealing with life and enjoying every moment it offered me. The key to this healing regimen is to not stay in bed forever, yet to allow yourself occasional pampering. There is no reason to feel guilt for caring for your needs. There is no reason to feel as if you can't take the time. Things can wait. If we do not care for our souls and do what is needed for our own happiness and joy, then we will never find what we are looking for. We will be searching endlessly if we do not allow ourselves time to find the answers within.

Chapter Twenty-Seven

Kathy began working for me on April 20, 1998 and what a blessing she has been. I am very fortunate that she came into my life. It is really amazing how things work out sometimes. I have always read about how people are brought our way when we need them. I needed someone like Kathy, and she was brought my way. I almost missed out on that opportunity because of my fears, but trusting in the situation enabled things to work out splendidly. She has become not only a wonderful co-worker but also a great friend.

~

My father and I continued to correspond every other week or so. We started out simply sharing factual information about each other, and then we progressed to more casual conversations about our current lives. I had not talked to him, in person, since the day at my uncle's funeral. All of our getting to know each other had been accomplished through the written word. Grandma Dean had been wanting to go visit him in Missouri again. It had been quite a few years since she had been there to see him. In the back of my mind I knew the time was coming when I would want to do more with my father than write him a letter. That time came more quickly than I had anticipated.

At the beginning of August I called grandma and asked her if she was up for a quick trip to see dad. She was thrilled and we tentatively set a four-day stretch towards the end of August for the trip. The next step was to find out if it was OK with my father. He had never mentioned anything about coming up to see me or inviting me down to see him. I didn't know if this was something he was interested in or not, but once again, there was a strong compulsion inside of me telling me to do this. So, I decided to take the responsibility to make it happen.

I had to call dad. I was frightened. What if he turned me down? What if the dates didn't work, then what? How would I remain brave when I knew it would hurt me if he declined? I went and sat upstairs on my bed with his phone number in my hand and stared at the phone. It was Sunday, August 2, about 3:00 in the afternoon. I picked up the phone, started to dial the number and hung up. I chickened out, was too nervous.

By 3:30 I knew if I was going to do this I had to do it now. I couldn't put it off any longer. With a deep breath and a quick prayer, I picked up the phone again, dialed the number and listened to it ring. After four rings he answered the phone.

Shyly I asked for Earl (even though I knew it was him). Once I told him who I was, there was an awkward moment of silence, during which neither of us really knew what to say. Then, after the usual small talk, I jumped into asking him if it was OK if grandma, Jeremy and I came to visit in a few weeks. He didn't even hesitate before he said yes. He checked his day-timer, and the chosen dates were clear for him. I said that was great, told him I'd let grandma know and said good-bye. It was a short phone conversation, and yet my nerves were shot. When he agreed to the visit, and seemed somewhat excited, I started to panic. Here I am getting myself into another situation. Now what was I going to do?

The next couple of weeks went by quickly. Dad wrote to me to confirm the visit and to say he was glad we were coming. I was nervous about imposing on him and his life, and at the same time I was looking forward to the trip. Sometimes I would get angry at myself for looking forward to it so eagerly; I didn't want to get my hopes up, but I couldn't help it. I knew it was going to be a difficult trip, and I was building myself up for it as the days flew by.

Things were slowly improving for my mother. After many years of experimenting with different medications, we finally found one that seemed to help her. I am happy to say that my mother is doing better now than she has for the past 28 years. We enjoy a tentative relationship. It certainly isn't a stereotypical mother-daughter relationship (if there is such a thing), but we can at least have a bit of a conversation with each other.

She lives in an apartment in Deerborne and spends her days at the Clark County Human Resources Building. There are different day programs for her to attend. She has made friends through those programs and it helps to pass the time for her.

Mom is not able to hold down a job. We have tried that and it just never worked. She does not own a vehicle, but she gets around pretty well using the local bus system. She tries to be involved in my life, and yet we don't have much in common. I call her every couple of weeks to check up on her, and I visit her when I can. She has no inkling of my relationship with my father or his side of the family. It would upset her greatly, and I see no need. My relationship with that side of the family does not interfere with her or my relationship with her. So, it's better left unsaid.

On August 14, one week before I was to head down to visit my dad, Pat, Jeremy and I went to have dinner with mom. She had invited us down for a visit; my birthday was coming soon, and she wanted to do this for me. We had to pick up Jeremy from camp, which was about two hours north of us, and then head down to mom's place, so it was a busy day. We were tempted to decline her invitation, but she had asked several times previously and we never had been able to make it. Since we were free that evening, we decided to go.

I was surprised that I enjoyed the evening with mom. Usually, I visit her more out of duty than desire. For too many years I harbored a deep-seated anger towards her and the things that she had said and done to us as children. Those are hard things to get over, though we must try.

Mom made a great meal, and she was actually talking and laughing. She seemed to be making a real effort towards her life now, and it was nice to see. When Pat and I were married, the only word he could use to describe mom was "medicated." It was true. She had no personality for years, because medicating her heavily was the only way we could help her maintain some equilibrium. The new medication seemed to make a world of difference.

It was a beautiful evening, and after dinner we took a drive around town, stopped at a park for a while and took a short hike. When it was time for us to head for home, we took mom back to her apartment; she got out of the back seat and came around to my window and gave me a kiss. This dinner was for my birthday and she gave me a birthday kiss.

It took me off guard. As we drove away I started to cry. I have always pushed her away from my life and I think (though I am just starting to realize it) she really hurt me emotionally when I was young.

In some ways I was the forgotten child. (I think every middle child says that.) It seemed as if mom always wanted me to be someone other than who I was. The Dean relatives have told me how much I am like my father. That seems odd to me—I had very little influence from him in my life, yet my personality is definitely more his than my mother's. I believe that I reminded my mother of my father when I was young. Maybe that is why we never got along. Maybe that is why she took so many things out on me and Tim rather than on the other two?

I cried most of that hour-long drive home. I felt sorry that my mother and I don't have a better relationship, but how could we? I have been more of a parent to her than she to me for so many years that I tend to think of myself as parentless. I think I was crying for all the lost years. I am sure my tears were also for my upcoming trip. I just didn't know what to expect, what to say or how to react.

~

It was August 17, three days before our trip to Missouri, and I was jumping out of my skin. I just wanted to leave right then and get it over with. I was terribly frustrated because there were lots of things I had to accomplish for upcoming programs, but I just couldn't get anything done. My mind and heart were focused on one thing and one thing only: my trip to see my dad.

Two nights before we were to leave, I couldn't sleep. I decided to get up, finally, at 3:00 A.M. and get some work done. I needed to calm down! I crawled back in bed a couple of hours later and slept for a while. We were leaving early the next morning, and I had to be well rested for the drive.

When we reached Missouri, we got settled into our hotel room and called my father to let him know we were in town. We went out to his home, had a short visit, and then went into town for dinner.

Initially I wasn't going to take Jeremy along, but I'm glad I did. It was a nice distraction for my dad and me. Grandma was so happy she was like a young girl. She had wanted my dad and me to know each other for so many years, and she was just thrilled that it was finally happening. I am glad she went with on this trip. Both she and Jeremy really helped my comfort level. After dinner we got a tour of the town that dad lived in and his church building, and then we went back out to his home until 10:00 or so. Here is a journal excerpt of mine from the next morning:

August 21, 5:45 A.M.: *"I am scared. Dad has been very nice to us—a little hyper, but yet worked very hard to make us feel comfortable. I can tell that grandma is enjoying her visit. Me—I am a mixed bag of emotions. I am starting to under-stand, Lord, why you sent me down here—for healing! I am just starting to get an inkling for how much hurt I experienced as a child, and the extent to which I either never dealt with it or covered it over with anger.*

Last night, while grandma, dad and his wife were in the kitchen eating dessert, I went and sat in the living room with Jeremy. During the tour of town I sat way in the back of the van and to this point, I really haven't said too much of any-thing. Dad asked me about my business; I smiled and said it was great. I want to trust him and like him; my heart is pulling in that direction and yet, I am afraid. I don't want to jump the gun because I am "awed" by my father figure.

While we were sitting in the living room, dad came in and sat in a chair directly across from me. I told him that grandma and Jeremy were excited to be here. (I couldn't tell him that I was, too—I tried and the words wouldn't come out.) He looked me in the eye and said, "Peggy, I am glad that you came down." I didn't respond.

Right now, I am working hard on not being jealous of the relationship that his stepchildren have with him. When he re-married, his wife had five children. Three of them were already grown and out of the house. The two younger ones were still home. The youngest, a girl, is the same age as I am.

I understand that if my father and I stay in touch after this visit, it is going to be a process of healing and gaining trust. Last night, as we bade one another good night, dad gave grandma a hug, then gave Jeremy a handshake and a hug. I stood back for some time, we both looked at each other, and then I gave in. I gave him a hug."

The best way to share the next two days is to simply let you read my journal. I think that sums it up the best:

Saturday, August 22, 7:00 A.M. *"Yesterday was a long, mentally exhausting day. I have still been calling him by his first name. I haven't been able to call him dad yet. At lunch, I had my first few moments alone with dad. He was silent and it was driving me nuts. I looked at him and said, "I can't tell if you're enjoying this or going through the motions because it's the right thing to do."*

He kind of grinned at me and said, "I am loving this and I wouldn't be doing it if I didn't want to." I still wasn't sure if he was telling me the truth, but, I decided to drop it at that point. We returned to silence.

Jeremy really seems to be taking a liking to this guy. He sat up in the front passenger seat the entire day. I sat in the back again—as far away as I could get. Grandma sat in the middle. Dad is doing anything he can to make Jeremy happy and comfortable. I suppose he is enjoying his time with his grandson. In fact, last night when Jeremy crawled into his sleeping bag he said, "Your dad is a nice guy and I like him."

After we did all the touring we could take in one day, we headed back to dad's house and hung out there for a while. We were all sitting in the living room visiting, and I needed a break. I got up, told everyone I was going outside for awhile and asked Jeremy to stay in the house; then I went and sat by the little swamp in dad's back yard. I sat and cried for 45 minutes or so, and finally decided I should go back in. I knew Jeremy would be worried and it turned out he was. I guess he came out twice looking for me.

The minute I went in, grandma asked Jeremy to go outside with her. I gave her a look that said "don't do this to me," but she ignored it. Come to think of it, I kept my sunglasses on when I came back in, so I suppose she didn't see the look I gave her. It was highly uncomfortable, with just dad and I sitting there in the living room, in silence, looking at each other. We talked a little bit about business and, to my great relief, grandma and Jeremy came back in.

Before dinner dad drove us to the town we lived in when I was five years old and in Kindergarten. After touring that little town, I felt thankful for the first time that dad had gotten me out of there when he did. I thought my home town was small, but it was a vast city compared to this.

Earlier this morning I was thinking I would like to leave today and go back home. That would definitely be the easy route. The most difficult part has been watching dad with his stepdaughter. They appear to have a great relationship. He calls her "honey." He is the only dad that she has known. Her dad died shortly after her mom married my dad and I suppose, in many ways, those kids replaced us—his own children. I am happy that he had some children to fill his life with.

I do want some time alone with him today. I want to know who he is, how he feels when he sees us, whether he has put all of us in his past. I haven't eaten much of anything over the past couple of days. My stomach has been too upset."

That Saturday, dad and I had a chance to talk. In fact, we talked for about three hours. I don't remember everything that was said, but I feel he was sincere and honest with me. The first thing I asked him was, "Does it bother you to see me?" As I said, I tend to be candid.

He sighed and said he was becoming more comfortable with me every day. He raved about Jeremy for a while and we both agreed that we were glad he had come. I went on to tell him that I didn't want to intrude into his life, that I didn't want him to be nice to me out of duty, and that it was difficult to see him with his other daughter. The last I said not in a jealous way—I was determined to be more mature than that—just in a way that recognized that she had what I had wanted and had missed out on.

We shared quite a bit of information that afternoon. Dad shared his viewpoint of the divorce and said he knew mom got very upset when he tried to see us and felt it was better if he tried not to intervene. He had tried several times to get information about us or to see us and was spurned. My mom's family wrote him a letter threatening arrest if he ever set foot in the state of Minnesota again. He said he was naïve and believed it, even though he didn't know what he would be arrested for. He knows his parents were treated badly by my mom and her family, but he couldn't do anything about it.

He told me that he has had some fulfillment with Shelly's kids, but that there always has been something missing. He then looked me straight in the eye, pointed his finger at me and said, "You are a part of that fulfillment and so are Nathan, Tim and Jessica."

He also talked about how tough the years were without knowing how we kids were doing. At this point in his life, he said, any relationship he has with us is "Grace from God, like dessert or frosting on a cake."

Sunday morning, the day we left, was not as easy as I had hoped it would be. We stopped by his church to catch him before his service began. He was with someone in his office. When he came out we all just kind of stood there. I wanted some time alone with him to say good-bye and I asked to see his office. Jeremy and I went in with him and looked around. I was about to say good-bye and I started to cry. I walked over to the corner of his office, with my back to him, and he sat and talked to Jeremy.

I had to straighten up and did. I thanked him for his hospitality and time. We hugged each other and I began to cry again. He hugged Jeremy about three times before we left the office. He said good-bye to grandma and we were on our way.

I was so glad that I took that trip. It was one of the best things I have ever done for myself. I really enjoyed my time with grandma. It gave us a few days to be together and create memories. It was bittersweet leaving dad. There was a side of me that just wanted to stay with my dad and another side of me that was anxious to get back home to my life and my husband.

For my birthday I received a bouquet of flowers from dad. I was so touched I just sat and cried. Man, I was getting tired of crying!

I was beginning to fully comprehend the sadness behind the whole situation. I wanted to get through the grieving process and on to that happiness part as quickly as I could, but I knew it would take time. A couple of days later I woke up at 2:00 in the morning crying some more. I felt sadness, anger, love for my dad, and yet, great fear. I felt extremely vulnerable, but I have learned that vulnerability is one of the most important stages to go through in this lifetime. It creates opportunities for personal growth.

Chapter Twenty-Eight

During the next couple of months, my emotions continued to waver. I was still afraid of the man who was my father, but not fearful enough to back away. I would go through stages of anger at him, then anger at my mom again, and then happiness because I had contact with him. I felt like a child who needed to be put back together again. What surprised me the most was the void that my dad filled. I hadn't even known there was a void there, yet, as our relationship grew its presence became very evident to me.

I found myself crying at wedding dances when the bride would dance with her father, crying at commercials that showed a family together, and crying when I saw a father playing with a young daughter. You name it, I cried at it—and, in some cases I'm still doing that today. Ask my family and they will tell you what a weeper I have become.

At one point in my life I looked at crying as a weakness. I have since discovered that it is healthy to cry and to allow ourselves to experience the emotions we feel. For too many years of my life, I did not allow myself to experience any of the emotions from my childhood, and that held me back from experiencing bigger and better things in life. For too many years I just tucked them away and didn't deal with them.

~

During the winter of 1998 my world seemed to be functioning relatively well. I was going through the healing process with my father, my mother was healthier than she had been in some time, my siblings and I still had our challenges, yet seemed to have come to an understanding about our roles in one another's lives. My son was becoming a young man before my very eyes, and my marriage was stronger than it had ever been.

With things going so well it would have been like me to be frightened into making some drastic change again, if for no other reason than to prevent myself from getting bored. I finally learned that it is good to have some stability in one's world. I have lived in Hastings for about eight years now, which is the longest I ever have resided in one spot; I consider it my home. This also has given Jeremy a place he can always refer to as his home town, one filled with fond memories, regardless of where life takes him.

~

In the spring of 1999 I decided I wanted to see my father again. I sent a note inviting him to come up and visit later in spring or early summer. I wanted my dad to see my life this time. We set a few days in mid-June aside for his visit. Preparing for that was another anxious time in my life.

Grandma Dean had not been feeling well, but she, too, was looking forward to dad's visit. Grandma was always elated to see me and even more so to see my father and me together.

On June 14 I told my mother-in-law that my father was coming to visit. She was surprised, to say the least. Pat's parents, my in-laws, have been wonderful influences in my life, and in Jeremy's. They have become like parents to me in many ways. It is comforting to have people who look out for me and my family, to call for advice and wisdom when needed, and who love me for who I am.

The profound thought is, if I had maintained my original set of chips on my shoulder, I wouldn't have had this great blessing—Pat's family—come into my world. Sure, Pat and I may still have been married, but I would not have allowed his family into my heart. I am glad that I matured and realized that a close, loving family is a good thing.

The few days before the visit I kept repeating to myself, "I expect good things to happen, I expect good things to happen, I expect good things to happen."

The above phrase has had a great calming effect for me in many instances of my life. Most of the stress that we encounter, the challenges that we experience, worries that we have, are all circling around in our minds. The key is to gain control of those thoughts and utilize them in a positive fashion.

We have two choices, each and every day of our lives: we can either expect the best or expect the worst. That's it; we can look at life in a positive fashion or a negative one. I have learned to choose the former one; I have trained myself always to think positively or to believe that something good will come out of every event in my life. Even if it takes me 20 years to see it, something good will always come out of every situation, if you want it to.

On June 17 Jeremy and I were to meet dad down in Lynden. I still felt vulnerable around him, but I was more confident since he was in my part of the country this time. I actually felt more confident that day than I had the week prior to his visit. I can get myself incredibly worked up about things, especially matters that affect my soul, and was glad that we were meeting at grandma's. She has a comforting affect on me.

We arrived at the apartment building, walked up the steps to the second floor where grandma lived, knocked on the door and walked right in. Dad got up to give us a hug and welcome us. I went over and gave grandma a hug and a kiss. We all sat and visited for a couple of hours. Jeremy sat right next to dad on the couch; I sat as far away as possible. It must have been my defense mechanisms. After dinner, Jeremy and I returned to Hastings. Dad was going to meet us the following morning, at our house.

Chapter Twenty-Nine

Friday morning, June 18, at about 10:15 A.M., dad arrived at our home on Maple Street. I had gotten up very early that morning. At least this time, I was home and could do something with my energy. I had worked on laundry, gone to the gym and picked up around the house. I knew it was worthless trying to work on business because I was too nervous. My stomach was in knots again.

We had decided that dad would stay overnight and just take off early in the morning from here. My thoughts were racing: What if he didn't like me once we spent time together? What if I didn't like him? What would we talk about? His acceptance of me was more important than I was willing to admit.

Once he arrived, I was fine. We gave him a tour of our house and decided to go visit the Mall of America. He had never been there before, and it is pretty spectacular. We were gone from about 11:00 until 4:30 that afternoon. After wandering around the Mall we decided to head back towards Hastings. I drove him around town to show him how it had changed since we had lived there together many years earlier. We all enjoyed the afternoon, and actually had fun.

I was in a bit of a state of shock that this was actually taking place. Never in my wildest dreams would I have imagined my dad and I spending a day together just kind of bumming around. Our conversation throughout the day was somewhat superficial, yet as the day wore on, I think the two of us felt more comfortable discussing certain things. He asked about my siblings and their families. I asked him what his life was like while we lived in Hastings.

When we got back to my home I showed him a few pictures of me as I was growing up. We talked about the divorce and what happened afterwards. There were a few tender moments. He recalled how he had nothing to remember us kids by. After he left our family, he went back to Missouri. Everything was with mom: the pictures, the memories, the kids. All he had were his clothes.

Pat had to work that day, and I am kind of glad that he did. It allowed Jeremy and me to be alone with my father. After Pat came home, we made dinner and went out in our backyard for one of our backyard bonfires. It was a nice relaxing evening. A couple of the neighbors stopped by to meet my dad, and Pat's parents also came over. About 10:30 we headed in for the night. Dad had a long drive ahead of him the next day.

There are times in our lives when the timing of events is perfect. I would say this was one of them. As I got out of my chair that Saturday morning, and prepared to get on with my day, I realized that things are the way they are meant to be, and that even though there were lots of years of hurt and pain, it is all behind me now and I can finally move on.

As I walked to the bathroom to shower and get dressed, I realized that things would have probably been different for me if I had the tiniest inkling that my father loved me. I know it now, but I didn't know it then. Things may have been different if I could have had some contact with my father and his family over the years. Each step I took over my lifetime, was in an effort to improve things. It didn't always turn out for the better, but I learned some valuable lessons:

1. **Accept who you are and your current position in life.**

   The first step towards improvement is awareness. Once we become aware of a situation, we then need to accept it with complete maturity. Take responsibility for your own life, even if it hurts a little. Make a vow, beginning today, that you, and only you, are responsible for your future happiness. Don't fight the acceptance phase. Without it, you will go no further.

2. **Reflect on your past and the patterns that have been developed.**

   Grab pen and paper to "empty out" all your emotions and thoughts about your past. What are your earliest childhood memories? Are they positive or negative? If they are negative, what can you learn from them? Take a trip down memory lane and look, objectively, at your path. Are there any negative patterns or habits that stand out? Is there something that you keep avoiding? What is one thing you can start doing differently, today, to improve your journey?

3. **Expect good things to happen.**

   As long as we expect good things to happen, we will be looking for them and will be more likely to see them when they are right in front of us. Time and time again, it has been proven to me that something good does come out of every tragedy. We just don't see the "good" immediately. It takes time, but it always works out.

There very well may have been some good things that happened in my world when I was growing up; there may have been some people who really did care for me and I didn't see them. I didn't expect to see them.

4. Let go of the negative influences.

That is a challenging venture. There are so many negative people in the world that I sometimes wonder what life is all about. It is easy to remain in a negative "crowd" and yet, if you are interested in becoming more than you currently are, this may be the missing link.

It has been fascinating to see how different people who have known me over the years have reacted as I have followed my personal journey of growth. Unfortunately, some of those people are no longer in my life. I haven't always received support for my desire to grow and become all that I can be. I haven't always received encouraging remarks from those who perceive that I am leaving them behind. Sometimes, it forces them to look in the mirror and question their happiness and their ability to handle risk. Because so many people have left me in my lifetime, I have a difficult time saying good-bye to people, even when I know they are influencing me negatively. I have learned, though, that I have to watch out for myself and not always be the one who looks out for everyone else.

Begin to write down, each and every day, the following: " I am going to eliminate the negative out of my life today." A warning for you, when you do this, you will find that you have very little tolerance for negative influences and find yourself creating a whole new world of friends. However, in my own experience, if I hadn't rid myself of the negative influences, I would not have the wonderful group of people in my life that I do today.

5. Remain grateful.

Gratitude is one of the most important attributes to carry with you on a daily basis. We can choose either to be grateful or not. It is a choice and I have found that when I am grateful I seem to enjoy my day a little more, things don't stress me out as much, I have more peace in my world. We have so much to be thankful for every day of our lives, and yet sometimes I think we get so busy that we forget to be grateful. Each day remind yourself of one person you are grateful for, and be sure and tell them about it.

6. **Temper your expectations of life, and of others.**

This is where I sometimes get into trouble. I have such a drive to live my life the way God intends me to that it is challenging to realize that not everyone else feels that way. This is where that tool of being non-judgmental comes in. If I keep an open mind and stop judging other people and situations, it seems I have less conflict in my world, I don't worry as much, and my time and energy are spent in more useful ways.

7. **Incorporate the art of forgiveness.**

Forgive everyone and everything that is holding you back, that causes you anger or that has disappointed you in the past. Holding on to anger will only hurt you, not the other party. You only live once and you don't want to waste a single moment by dwelling on hurts from yesterday.

The most difficult person to forgive, typically is, yourself. It may seem virtually impossible and yet, it isn't. We just have to train ourselves to do it. Again, write down on a pad and paper everyone and everything you need to forgive, including your own mistakes. Keep doing this until it sinks in. Remind yourself that you cannot go back and change any events that took place, but you can have a brighter future due to the lessons learned.

8. **Trust the process.**

There are few things we can control in life, and sometimes we need to just let go of the outcome. Too many of us feel that we need to find "perfection" before we can truly be happy. Well, news alert, there is no such thing as perfection. Sure, for a fleeting moment you may feel that you have found it, but it won't last. Do the best you can with what you have and trust the rest to work out.

9. **Stop comparing yourself to others.**

It is unhealthy to look at others and feel envy. Envy is a terribly destructive emotion and I hate it when it wells up inside of me. When you look at someone and feel that you are not worthy, remind yourself that you are. We were all created equal, and each of us has the same opportunities ahead of us as the next person. For some of us it may be more difficult than for others, but that doesn't mean that we can't accomplish what we want to. Envy is an ugly emotion that can really hamper our development. Be happy for others and the success they experience. When others see your genuine happiness, they may be more inclined to help you when or if you need it.

10. Use the power of the written word.

I have stated countless times that the power of the written word is astonishing. When you find yourself feeling frightened or lacking in courage to do something, simply sit down and write out what those feelings are. The next step is to clarify what you hope to achieve; it is commonly referred to as an affirmation.

You can call it whatever you want. The idea is to put out on paper what you want to do or change or adjust. It is proven, time and time again, that if you can write out your wishes or dreams, that somewhere inside of you, you believe you can do it. Whether that belief is as small as your baby toe, if you can write it down, it shows belief in yourself. Continue to write it down until it comes true. Personal enrichment starts with desire, and that is not something that I can give you; it has to come from within.

As you write down your thoughts and emotions, you'll discover that, truly, all the solutions, or answers, that you're looking for are inside of you. You will see, quite logically, what you are feeling and you'll discover that, it doesn't matter if it is right or not. There is no right or wrong when it comes to our emotions. Many of us are hard on ourselves because of the way we feel at any given moment throughout the day. Grant yourself permission to experience what you need to, so you can get on with your life.

It is always scary to move on, or to take that leap of faith to follow your dreams and your heart's calling. Yet, in my experience it is very well worth it. Continue to write down your dreams and objectives and before you know it, they will be upon you!

In Closing

There you have it—my life story for all to see, judge and explore. As my friend Annie says, "Peggy, you have a lot of mileage for your 32 years." She is right. I have had a lot of hard lessons in my lifetime and yet, for some of us, that is the only way we learn. Upon reflection, I have come to realize that I wouldn't change anything from my past. After all, it has made me who I am today. I figure the best is yet to come.

That doesn't mean that I don't expect to continue to encounter challenges and disappointments. We all have them. The important issue is how are we going to do deal with them? Are we going to give up or continue on? Are we going to become bitter about what we are lacking, or grateful for what we have?

On September 8, 1999, my Grandma Dean passed away. She had brain cancer and, thankfully, didn't suffer for very long. She was a woman of courage, faith and love. While I really miss her, I also choose to be thankful for the short time we had together. Even though she is gone I can close my eyes and still feel the love she always gave me, see the smile on her face when I was around and hear the laughter in her voice when we talked on the phone. I hope I never lose that memory; it is a special one and I am going to do my best to keep it in my heart.

It is amazing how grandma did not pass away until after my father had been up here for a visit and we were well on our way to creating a solid relationship. When my Grandpa Dean died, I met my dad and his side of the family. When my Uncle Bill died, I had the opportunity to forge a relationship with my father. Grandma was in the hospital within two weeks of my father visiting me in my home. Once she entered the hospital, she was never the same again.

I had the opportunity to say good-bye to her the day before she passed away. We typically go away on Labor Day weekend, but due to Jeremy's first football game, we stayed home. We spent that Sunday at the State Fair, and when we arrived home there was a message that grandma was going downhill fast. I drove down there early that Monday morning, Labor Day. I had been down there once a week to visit her, and she did seem as if her time was nearing its end. I held her hand, told her how much I loved her and how happy I was to know her. She couldn't talk and yet seemed to understand what I was saying because she squeezed my hand. She squeezed my hand and wouldn't let go. I didn't want to sit and cry in front of her, so I pulled my hand away, kissed her on the top of her head and walked away. Within 48 hours she was gone.

I feel my brothers and sister really missed out by not knowing her. It is unfortunate when pride or hate or misunderstandings get in the way of relationships. All parties missed out due to Nathan, Tim and Jessica's ignorance regarding my father's family as it really was. I am thankful I chose to go down my own path.

Life is what you make it. It is there for the taking. I encourage you to grab onto it and make it whatever you want it to be.

Thank you for being a part of my life—if only through the written word. I wish, hope and pray that you find your life filled with peace, joy and happiness. Many Blessings.